Y

YORK NOTES

The Color Purple

Alice Walker

Notes by Neil McEwan

 Longman   York Press

We are grateful to David Higham Associates on behalf of the author, Alice Walker, for permission to reproduce extracts from *The Color Purple*, published in Great Britain by The Women's Press Limited, 1983

The right of Neil McEwan to be identified as Author of this Work has been asserted by him in accordance with the Copyright, Designs and Patents Act 1988

YORK PRESS
322 Old Brompton Road, London SW5 9JH

PEARSON EDUCATION LIMITED
Edinburgh Gate, Harlow,
Essex CM20 2JE, United Kingdom
Associated companies, branches and representatives throughout the world

First published 1998
Second impression 1999

ISBN 0–582–32909–4

Designed by Vicki Pacey
Phototypeset by Gem Graphics, Trenance, Mawgan Porth, Cornwall
Colour reproduction and film output by Spectrum Colour
Prodcued by Addison Wesley Longman China Limited, Hong Kong

CONTENTS

PART ONE

INTRODUCTION

HOW TO STUDY A NOVEL

Studying a novel on your own requires self-discipline and a carefully thought-out work plan in order to be effective.

- You will need to read the novel more than once. Start by reading it quickly for pleasure, then read it slowly and thoroughly.
- On your second reading make detailed notes on the plot, characters and themes of the novel. Further readings will generate new ideas and help you to memorise the details of the story.
- Some of the characters will develop as the plot unfolds. How do your responses towards them change during the course of the novel?
- Think about how the novel is narrated. From whose point of view are events described?
- A novel may or may not present events chronologically: the time-scheme may be a key to its structure and organisation.
- What part do the settings play in the novel?
- Are words, images or incidents repeated so as to give the work a pattern? Do such patterns help you to understand the novel's themes?
- Identify what styles of language are used in the novel.
- What is the effect of the novel's ending? Is the action completed and closed, or left incomplete and open?
- Does the novel present a moral and just world?
- Cite exact sources for all quotations, whether from the text itself or from critical commentaries. Wherever possible find your own examples from the novel to back up your opinions.
- Always express your ideas in your own words.

This York Note offers an introduction to *The Color Purple* and cannot substitute for close reading of the text and the study of secondary sources.

How you read *The Color Purple* is up to you. A feminist, an African American, a civil rights activist, a folklorist, a religious believer and a poet might read with attention to different aspects of the novel. Alice Walker, who is all these things, also stresses the pleasure and power of story-telling, whatever the commitments that inspired a story. As we shall see, a wide range of interest is to be found in what has proved a very powerful story indeed.

REPUTATION

However it appeared to its first readers in 1982, it is hard to approach the novel today without having its reputation in mind. *The Color Purple* almost immediately became a bestseller, a modern classic and a centre of fierce controversy. Winning the American Book Award and the Pulitzer Prize (never before awarded to a **black** woman), it remained on the New York Times Bestseller List for over a year. Steven Spielberg's film of 1985 enlarged both the readership and the heated debate that already surrounded the book in the United States.

Some readers who share Alice Walker's outlook have welcomed the commercial success as an opportunity to spread their views. Others have feared that the desire to write a bestseller may have compromised the author's principles. Some critics, for example, have felt that the **realism** of the early part of the story is sacrificed in favour of the happy ending (see Critical History).

The scale of the book's success does seem to have been helped by its double appeal. It can be read as a shocking and subversive assault on 'masculine values', but at the same time it is a romantic and sentimental story of two poor sisters who triumph over adversity. Commitment to a cause and popular story-telling can act as a powerful combination, and Walker's opponents were quick to try to counter the novel's influence.

WOMANISM

Alice Walker's strongest commitment is, in her own term, 'womanist'. At the heart of her story a man is denouncing his wife: 'You black, you pore, you ugly, you a woman. Goddam, he say, you nothing at all' (p. 176). The whole novel can be read as an attack on the assumptions behind these words of Albert to the heroine Celie. Its central theme, that blackness and womanhood are rich and beautiful endowments, is womanist, and aggressively so.

A womanist manifesto is set out as a foreword to Walker's book of essays, *In Search of Our Mothers' Gardens: Womanist Prose* (1983). The term is defined under four heads: (i) a black feminist; (ii) 'a woman who loves other women, sexually and/or nonsexually' (and sometimes also loves men 'sexually and/or nonsexually'), who prefers women's culture, and is 'committed to survival and wholeness of entire people, male and female'; (iii) 'Loves music. Loves dance. Loves the moon. *Loves* the Spirit. Loves love and food and roundness. Loves struggle. *Loves* the Folk. Loves herself. *Regardless*'; (iv) 'Womanist is to feminist as purple to lavender'.

The Color Purple can be read as a celebration of this creed. Celie lives though many misfortunes at the hands of men, including rapes and beatings, and survives to grow into mature and independent womanhood, helped by her love of and sexual relationship with another woman, the singer Shug Avery. In Celie's eyes, and the reader's, Shug becomes a heroic figure, a queen who deserves to be clad in royal purple. For sympathetic readers it can seem, in the words of one feminist critic, 'the perfect emancipation novel' (see Critical History). Celie is freed from poverty and degradation, from marriage and from all forms of **patriarchy**.

Not all critics have been sympathetic. In the United States especially, there were strong objections to the lesbian theme and to the remorseless depiction of acts of male violence against women in a novel about black people. Some American critics argued that Alice Walker threatened to divide the black community and detract from the struggle against racism. Her attacks on all forms of male aggression, physical and cultural, found eager defenders, and she has published many accounts of her views on the novel and responses to criticism.

LITERARY QUALITIES

Some admirers and detractors are so concerned with social issues that they treat the novel as a battleground for debate rather than a work of literature with strengths and weaknesses of composition. This is to neglect the fact that *The Color Purple* raises interesting literary questions too. Various traditions in American literature are combined. One is the **slave narrative**, dating from the eighteenth century. Although the period of history covered in the novel is two generations later than the age of slavery, Celie and her sister Nettie are virtually enslaved in the early part of the story, and they live in a society still suffering from slavery's aftermath.

Another is the literature of black protest, from the days of slavery onwards. Albert's words quoted above, 'You black, you pore, you ugly, you a woman' and Celie's reply, 'I'm pore, I'm black ... But I'm here' (p. 176), are reminiscent of the ironic rhetoric of Sojourner Truth (1797–1883), the formidable abolitionist and women's rights activist (see Further Reading). Alice Walker is also one of the best known of the group of modern African-American women novelists of the South who have emerged during the last twenty-five years and who share an admiration for the work of Zora Neale Hurston (?1901–60). These and other elements in Walker's reading are discussed later (see Literary Background).

History

The Color Purple can be read as a historical novel. The story begins in the early years of the twentieth century and, following the life of Celie, covers several decades of life in the American South, emphasising the hardships and joys of black people, and especially of black women at the hands of men. The story of Nettie, a missionary in Africa, surveys the colonial period with an equally feminist stress on the oppression not only of Africans by Europeans but also of African women by African men. Early-twentieth-century history at home and abroad, the novel asserts, shows the sorry mess that men have made of the world.

History in Alice Walker, and especially in this novel, aims to be unconventional, and inclined to mock at masculine conceptions of Great Men. *In Search of Our Mothers' Gardens* (1983) records how the 'germ' of the story was a remark about a pair of female drawers. Walker remembers how 'a black male critic ... said he'd heard I might write a historical novel someday, and went on to say, in effect: Heaven protect us from it.' She laughed over this because 'womanlike (he would say), my "history" starts not with the taking of lands, or the birth, battles and deaths of Great Men, but with one woman asking another for her underwear' (pp. 355–6).

It could be argued that one of the novel's strengths is its amalgam of historical survey with an everyday perspective, focused on underwear and kitchen floors, and the feelings of the people closest to such real things. The way that Celie's character is developed through the evolving language and style of her letters is also impressive. As Celie becomes more literate, she grows in confidence, raising her head in the world (see Textual Analysis).

'THE SPIRIT'

Celie begins by writing to God. A new preface to the 1992 (tenth anniversary) edition of *The Color Purple* complains that critics have neglected the theme of religious faith. Celie and Nettie are deeply pious women, and Alice Walker conveys their feelings from memories of her own Christian upbringing. She has rejected Christianity (calling herself 'a born-again pagan') in favour of belief in 'the Spirit' (to whom the novel is dedicated), and maintains that religion should be taken out of churches and returned to nature. Shug Avery teaches a similar, **pantheist** faith in the novel, and Celie comes to accept it.

Some feminists may agree with Shug that traditional Christian language and **imagery** are misleading where they imply that God is an old white man. Others may feel that Walker is a better poet than theologian, and that the evocative symbol of the colour purple enriches the novel more effectively than vague talk about the Spirit. With Alice Walker, there is always plenty of opportunity to disagree (see Theme on Religious Belief).

BEARINGS

For feminists, even for those who distance themselves from Alice Walker's position, this novel has already become a classic. Readers other than feminists are likely to be drawn into the story by the life and wit of her writing. Celie's people are all excellent talkers, and she has an amazing way with words. This is a very polemical book, but it has many other qualities, polemic aside, as we shall see, including a distinctive warmth and tenderness, and a disarming sense of fun.

PART TWO

SUMMARIES

The *Color Purple* was published in the United States by Harcourt Brace Jovanovich, New York, 1982. It was published in Great Britain by The Women's Press, London, 1983, and has been constantly reprinted ever since. A new preface was added in 1992 to mark the tenth anniversary. This Note is based on the text of the British edition.

The letters are not numbered in any edition of the novel. For study purposes it is very convenient to number the letters, although in writing about the novel it should never be implied that they figure in the text. Students numbering the letters 1–90 for use with these summaries must remember that each letter begins on a fresh page. Letters quoted within letters are not to be numbered.

SYNOPSIS

The story begins in the first decade of the twentieth century. The setting is rural Georgia, and the characters are black Americans. Celie (who is never given a surname) is fourteen years old. Her mother is mentally disturbed. We find out later that this is due to the death of her father, lynched twelve years ago by white business rivals. Celie thinks that her mother's second husband, Alphonso, is her father. She has a younger, much loved sister, Nettie, and numerous small half-brothers and sisters. When Alphonso rapes her she writes a letter to God, asking for a 'sign', because she cannot understand what has happened. This begins a sequence of fifty-one letters from Celie to God, written at intervals over a period of more than thirty years.

Celie's mother dies. Alphonso takes away the two children, a girl and a boy, that Celie bears him. He threatens to rape Nettie, but Celie intervenes, offering herself in her sister's place. When Celie is about nineteen, Alphonso marries her to a local farmer. Celie calls her husband Mr — (afraid to use his first name, Albert). Her husband treats her brutally, often beating her, and she works in his house and on his farm almost as a slave. One day she sees her daughter, now aged six, and the woman who, with her clergyman-husband, has adopted the child, who is called Olivia. Nettie comes to live with Celie but is soon obliged to flee from the advances of Mr ——. Celie advises Nettie to seek out the couple who have adopted Olivia.

Mr —— has four children by his former wife and Celie cares for them. The eldest boy, Harpo, grows up and marries Sofia, a strong, independent-minded woman who loves, but refuses to live in subjection to, her husband. She retaliates very effectively when Harpo tries to beat her. Celie is at first envious of Sofia's free spirit, but they are reconciled after a quarrel and become friends.

Celie and Mr —— have one thing in common: both are infatuated with the famous singer Shug Avery. Mr —— has been Shug's lover, and they have had children together. Celie has only seen her in a photograph. When Shug falls ill, Mr —— takes her in and Celie nurses her. Celie is sexually attracted by Shug and devoted to her, and through her devotion they become friends. When Shug says 'Albert', Celie realises that she had forgotten his first name. Sofia has wearied of Harpo's bullying, and goes to live with one of her sisters with their five children. Harpo converts the house into a jukejoint: a bar with music and dancing. Shug sings there, dedicating a song to 'Miss Celie'.

Sofia returns one evening to the jukejoint. She quarrels with Harpo's girlfriend, Mary Agnes, nicknamed Squeak, and knocks her down. A few days later she quarrels with the wife of the white mayor and, when he strikes her, Sofia knocks him down. She is arrested, badly beaten and sentenced to twelve years' imprisonment. After three years she is placed in the mayor's household as a prisoner-maid to his wife Miss Millie. Shug leaves Celie and Albert, and tours the country as a singer, growing famous and rich.

Years go by. One Christmas, Shug returns with a husband, a toothy, vulgar man called Grady. When Grady and Albert stay out all night drinking, Shug and Celie share a bed, for warmth. Celie tells of how Alphonso abused her. Shug comforts her and they make love.

Shug discovers that Nettie has been writing to her sister for more than twenty years and that Albert has been hiding the letters. She and Celie find bundles of letters in a trunk. A sequence of these letters to Celie now tells us what has become of Nettie. The preacher, Samuel, and his wife Corrine, the couple who adopted Olivia and Celie's other child Adam, have taken Nettie into their household, and she has gone with them as a missionary to Africa. She describes conditions among the Olinka tribe where they have lived and worked ever since. The Olinka are a poor but independent people until the building of a road and the introduction of rubber plantations, to benefit faraway foreign interests, destroys their way of life.

Corrine notices how closely the children resemble Nettie and is jealous, supposing Nettie to have been Samuel's lover. She accepts the truth only on her deathbed. Nettie now learns that Samuel was formerly acquainted with Alphonso, and knows the facts about the sisters' parentage. Nettie and Samuel go to England to try and help the Olinka, and there they marry. Unfortunately, their efforts on behalf of the Olinka are unsuccessful, and they return disappointed. Adam falls in love with an African girl called Tashi, and becomes distressed because she has her face scarred in a traditional ceremony. Missionary work becomes unfeasible in this part of Africa, and the family hope to return to America.

Nettie's letters are interspersed with letters Celie writes to her. Celie is overjoyed to find that Alphonso is not their father. Shug talks to Celie about religion, and persuades her that God is not to be pictured as a wise old (white) man, but worshipped as a power in Nature and a spiritual force within us. Sofia is released from service in the mayor's house. Mary Agnes becomes a professional singer. She goes off to Panama with Grady, and Sofia returns to Harpo. Celie announces that she means to leave Albert and go to live with Shug in Memphis. She curses her husband and he denounces her as a poor, ugly, black woman, that is to say 'nothing at all'. Celie proves him wrong when she goes to Memphis, where she runs a successful business called 'Folkspants, Unlimited', and lives happily with Shug. It is Albert who goes into a decline, having to be nursed back to health by Harpo. He only recovers when he returns the remainder of Nettie's letters to Celie, and is thus freed from his wife's curse.

Alphonso dies. Celie and Nettie inherit land and a business, formerly their father's and willed to them, but withheld by Alphonso. Celie is heartbroken when Shug falls for Germaine, a young man in her band, and tours the country with her new boyfriend. Sofia's sixth child (not Harpo's), Henrietta, becomes sick, and Celie nurses her. There is a false report of

Nettie's death in the Atlantic (by this time the Second World War has started). Shug leaves Germaine and returns to Celie. Albert is now a reformed character; he has even taken up sewing. He and Celie have friendly talks; she even mentions his name, but there is no chance of a revival of their marriage. Celie tells him frankly that she has always found men physically unappealing.

The last letter sees the reconciliation of all the principal characters. Nettie and Samuel, Adam and his wife Tashi, with Olivia, come safely home, and Celie has a family at last. This, the ninetieth letter, is addressed to 'Dear God. Dear stars, dear trees, dear sky, dear peoples. Dear Everything', and offers thanks for happiness at last.

Time Scheme
Dates are approximate (see Dating Events)

Letter 1 **1904–5**	Celie is aged fourteen	**Letter 31** **1922–3**	Sofia leaves Harpo
Letter 2 **1905–6**	Death of Mama	**Letters 37–41** **1924**	Sofia is sent to prison
Letter 9 **1910**	Celie marries Albert	**Letter 43** **1927**	Sofia becomes a nursemaid
Letter 10 **1911**	Celie sees Olivia, aged six	**Letter 45** **1934**	Shug, married to Grady, comes for Christmas
Letter 11 **1912**	Nettie runs away	**Letter 49** **1935**	Celie receives her first letter from Nettie
Letters 54–5 **1913–14**	Nettie arrives in Africa	**Letter 74** **1936**	Sofia is released from prison
Letter 18 **1917**	Harpo marries Sofia	**Letter 80** **1939**	Nettie marries Samuel
Letter 22 **1921**	Shug comes to stay with Albert and Celie	**Letters 88–90** **1941–2**	Resolution

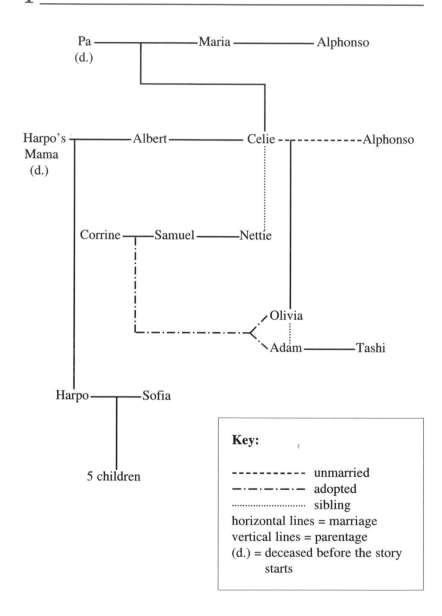

Pa — Maria — Alphonso
(d.)

Harpo's — Albert — Celie - - - - - - - - - Alphonso
Mama
(d.)

Corrine — Samuel — Nettie

Olivia
Adam — Tashi

Harpo — Sofia

5 children

Key:

- - - - - - - - - unmarried
— . — . — . — adopted
.... sibling
horizontal lines = marriage
vertical lines = parentage
(d.) = deceased before the story
        starts

LETTER 1   'Dear God, What is happening to me?' Celie has been
             raped by her stepfather

A fourteen-year-old girl is writing to God because she has no one else to
confide in. She does not give her name; we learn in Letter 7 that she is
called Celie. The reader understands from what she says that Celie has been
raped by a man called Alphonso ('Fonso'), apparently living with her
mother, who has been resisting Alphonso's advances and was away visiting
a doctor at the time of the rape. We learn in Letter 6 that Celie believes the
man to be her father. [He eventually turns out to be her stepfather.] She is
shocked and distressed. She hopes that God will send her 'a sign'. Her
mother, she says, is too ill to live long.

> The **point of view** is that of a naive first-person narrator. The girl
> describes what happened to her in blunt but innocent terms. It is
> obvious that she does not have a concept of rape or understand the
> probable consequences.

> We notice non-standard features of language indicating southern
> American dialect speech, especially in the use of verbs, but many
> sentences are normally formed, including, for example, the first three
> (see Language and Style).

> The point of view remains that of Celie confiding in God until Letter
> 52. Other voices are heard as Celie remembers them, her mother's,
> and Fonso's, here, those of Mr — and other characters later.

Lucious Lucius
Macon a city in Georgia
kine kind

LETTER 2   A year later, Celie is pregnant for a second time and fears
             that Alphonso will kill this baby too

This must be a year later, because Celie is pregnant for the second time.
The birth of the first baby astonished Celie. When her mother asked who
was responsible, she said that God was. Alphonso took the baby away and,
she believes (wrongly, as we find out in Letter 10), killed it in the woods.
Celie told her mother that 'God took it'. Her mother has since died, in
agony and rage, and it seems that Alphonso felt some genuine grief at her

death. Celie tells God that she fears Alphonso will kill her next baby too. Meanwhile she has to keep house, and act as nanny to all her smaller brothers and sisters.

> Contrasting this summary with the text of the second letter shows the extent to which the reader is obliged to interpret the narrator's anxious, urgent messages to God. She assumes that God will understand everything. We need to work out the sequence of events.

LETTER 3   **Alphonso is now eyeing Celie's younger sister Nettie**

More months have passed. Alphonso has not killed Celie's second baby, but sold it to a childless couple living some distance away. Alphonso tells her she is 'evil', disobedient and 'indecent' because she has milk running down her body and no proper clothes. He does nothing to help her. She hopes he will marry again soon. He is looking lustfully at Nettie, Celie's younger sister. Nettie is afraid, but Celie means to protect her, God willing.

Monticello a town in Georgia

LETTER 4   **Alphonso has married again. A widower is interested in Nettie**

Celie is reluctant to give Alphonso a name, usually writing only 'he', but in this letter she calls him 'Pa'. Pa has brought home a new wife, a teenage girl of about Celie's age. This girl seems to like her husband, but is bewildered by her new duties in a house with so many young children. A widower with three children is interested in Nettie, and he visits her every Sunday. Celie calls him Mr —. His wife was killed 'by her boyfriend coming home from church'. Celie is sure that Nettie will do better to continue attending classes at the local school, rather than submit to such a marriage.

> It is not until Letter 82 that Celie learns that Alphonso is not her father.

Gray a town in Georgia
in the same shape of the same age and build
more than a notion a serious undertaking

LETTER 5   Celie is not attracted by men, only by women. She hopes to
save Nettie from Alphonso

Alphonso has beaten Celie, she reports to God, for winking at a boy in
church. She did not wink, and she does not look at men. She looks at
women instead. She finds women more attractive because they do not
frighten her. She mentions that God might be surprised at this, because her
mother used to curse at her so much. She denies that she feels angry with
her mother, blaming her Pa's lies for her mother's death. When she sees Pa
eyeing Nettie, she stands in his way. She advises Nettie to marry her
admirer, because that will save her from Pa. She says that Nettie may be
able to enjoy one more year of her youth before the pregnancies begin.
Celie does not expect to become pregnant again.

story lies

LETTER 6   Alphonso does not allow Mr — to marry Nettie. Celie is
attracted by a photograph of the singer Shug Avery

Mr — asks Alphonso for Nettie's 'hand in marriage'. Alphonso refuses on
the grounds that Nettie is too young and Mr — has too many children. His
last wife, furthermore, died in scandalous circumstances. There are further
scandalous rumours about a liaison between Mr — and a woman called
Shug Avery.

Shug Avery interests Celie and her 'new mammy', who manages to
obtain a picture. Shug turns out to be a beautiful woman, rouged and
dressed in furs, with a certain sadness about the eyes. The photograph
shows her in front of a motor-car. Celie is fascinated by this romantic
image. She stares at the photograph every night, and dreams about Shug –
'dressed to kill', and dancing and laughing.

somethin tail animal fur

LETTER 7   Alphonso offers Celie to Mr — in place of Nettie

We learn Celie's name, and that she is now nearly twenty. While her new
mother is sick, Celie has to protect Nettie from Pa by offering herself
instead. To make herself more alluring, she dresses herself up as well as she
can. She succeeds in rescuing her sister, although she also suffers another
beating and sexual assault for her effrontery.

Mr — calls again, terrifying Nettie. Alphonso, however, refuses to part with Nettie, saying that he means to make a schoolteacher of her when she has had some more education. In her place he offers Celie. He tells Mr — that although she is ugly and not a virgin, Celie has two advantages: she works hard, and she is not able to bear any more children. Obliged to listen to this account of herself, Celie finds consolation in gazing into the sad but powerful eyes of Shug Avery in the treasured picture. Alphonso offers to give Celie a dowry: her own linen and a cow. Mr — is left to consider this handsome offer.

We learn Celie's name by chance when she mentions how Alphonso spoke of her. Celie's avoidance of it up to now suggests her low self-esteem. Her unwillingness to name men, saying only 'he' or Mr —, suggests her negative feelings about them. She names Nettie and Shug repeatedly and possessively.

Alphonso's contempt for women appears in his references to 'a fresh one'. He speaks of Celie and of his wife as though of animals or slaves.

horsehair worn as a hair-piece

trampy behaving like a prostitute

God done fixed her it is believed that she is now infertile

it bees it is. Shug's eyes seem to say that insults from men are an inevitable part of life

crib barn

LETTER 8   **Mr — agrees to marry Celie. Celie and Nettie are studying hard**

Spring has gone by, and Mr — has decided to marry Celie. She thinks only of Nettie, whom she hopes to be able to save from Alphonso. Perhaps this will be easier, she tells herself, when she is married to Mr — since he obviously still prefers Nettie. The sisters may be able to run away together. Meanwhile they are working hard at Nettie's schoolbooks, trying to make themselves well enough educated to survive in the world on their own if they do run away. Celie has not been to school since the time of her first pregnancy (five years ago), since her love of school means nothing to Mr —. He ignored Nettie's pleas on her sister's behalf, and those of the teacher, Miss Beasley, dismissing her as a garrulous spinster. Miss Beasley gave up her attempts to intervene when she saw that Celie was pregnant.

Mr — comes to make a final inspection of Celie. She has to turn about before him while he sits on his horse and Alphonso reads his newspaper. Mr — agrees to take Celie as his wife only when he is reassured that the cow is still included in the bargain.

Celie's ironic remark on how flat the world looks to her is a sign of her improving powers of self-expression. The description of Celie standing before Mr — while he looks her up and down is one of many which imply that Celie and Nettie are treated like slaves (see Theme on Slavery).

Columbus ... Santomareater Christopher Columbus (1451–1506) sailed from Spain in 1492 with three ships: the *Santa Maria*, the *Pinta*, and the *Niña*

Indians ... queen Columbus took slaves back from the New World as one of his gifts for King Ferdinand V and Queen Isabella of Spain, who had financed his voyage

run off at the mouth talks too much

bout the ground ... flat that the earth is a sphere

drug out exhausted

nary one of them not one of the children

LETTER 9 **Married to Mr — and lying in bed with him, Celie thinks about Shug Avery**

Celie is married. On her wedding night Mr —'s eldest boy, a twelve-year-old, throws a stone which cuts her head. His mother died in his arms, and he wants no stepmother. It turns out that Mr — has four children, all hard work to look after. Celie lies in bed with Mr —, thinking about how to keep Nettie safe. Then she thinks about Shug Avery, who perhaps used to enjoy what Mr — is now doing to her. This thought makes her put an arm around her husband.

We discovered how the child's mother was killed by her boyfriend in Letter 4. The brutal behaviour of Mr — is reinforced by the image of Celie's bandaged head on this loveless wedding night.

LETTER 10 **Celie finds her daughter Olivia**

Celie sees a little girl bearing a strong resemblance to herself and to Alphonso, walking in town behind the woman who has adopted her (or bought her). She is about the right age to be the baby taken from Celie six years ago. Celie's heart tells her that this is her first child.

Olivia's new mother is buying cloth in the store. Celie approaches and finds out that the new father is a clergyman. The storekeeper speaks contemptuously to both women (in a manner that suggests he must be white) and they leave. Since the Reverend Mr — has not yet arrived, they sit in Celie's husband's wagon to wait. As they talk we learn for the first time that Celie's husband is a handsome man. She admits that men all look alike to her. Her daughter's adoptive parents have named the little girl Pauline, but given her the pet name of Olivia. The Reverend Mr — makes a brief appearance, a large man. Olivia's new mother has a lively sense of fun. When Mr — returns, he finds to his annoyance that Celie is bursting with laughter.

'Girl' is a contemptuous form of address to a black woman. See Letter 71 for a comment on the offence this incident causes (see Theme on Slavery).

long hind along behind
daidies nappies
bolt a large roll of cloth, straight from the loom
clam climbs
don't hit on much don't look smart
git it understand the word-play on 'hospitality'

LETTER 11   Nettie runs away from Alphonso and comes to stay with Celie and Mr —

Nettie comes to stay with Celie and her husband, having run away from Alphonso. Her presence is a comfort to Celie, to whom she passes on what she has learned at school. Nettie urges Celie to control the children with a firmer hand, and to try to fight in the battle of life; Celie says she only knows how to survive. She still cares more about Nettie than about herself, and is afraid that her sister's talents will be lost if she has to marry a man like Mr —.

Mr — has agreed to let Nettie stay because he hopes to seduce her. When she resists his advances, he says she must leave. There is an emotional parting. Celie advises her to seek the help of the Reverend

Mr —'s wife – the only woman Celie has ever seen allowed to handle money for herself. Celie says she will not be alone so long as she can spell G-o-d. They agree to write to each other. But after Nettie has gone, no letters arrive.

We learn why no letters arrive from Nettie in Letter 50: Mr — intercepts and hides them. This is one of the **melodramatic** features of the plot.

they mean they are inconsiderate
to make miration over to make a fuss about showing admiration

letter 12   Two sisters come to stay

Carrie and Kate, two of Mr —'s sisters, come to stay. They praise Celie's housekeeping warmly, stressing this as a duty of all married women, sadly neglected by Mr —'s previous wife, Annie Julia. She had not wanted to marry Mr — at all; once married, he continued his pursuit of his former lover, Shug Avery, with no regard for his wife's feelings. Celie is a wife to be valued: tireless in keeping house, cooking and tending the children.

Kate comes again, this time alone, and urges her brother to buy his wife some clothes, instead of keeping her in rags. When Kate takes her to buy the clothes, Celie daydreams about Shug Avery. She considers what colour of dress Shug Avery would wear. Shug is like a queen to Celie, and so she thinks it would be purple, the royal colour, with maybe a little red to brighten it. But Mr — is unlikely to waste his money on such expensive colours, so Celie settles for blue, and is overcome with the dress – the first that has ever been made for her.

Kate tells the eldest boy, Harpo, to help Celie with the chores. Harpo refuses, saying that such work is only fit for women. When Kate insists, Harpo tells Mr —, who sends her home. Kate offers Celie the advice she has already received from Nettie: she should learn to fight for herself. Celie says nothing, but thinks that by doing as she is told, she will at least stay alive. Nettie tried to fight, and now (so Celie thinks) she is dead.

The novel is historically accurate in making black as well as white characters use terms such as 'nigger', as in 'a trifling nigger' meaning 'a silly boy' in this letter.

LETTER 12 continued

a nasty 'oman bout the house a poor housekeeper
newmonya pneumonia

LETTER 13   Harpo learns about how to treat a wife

Harpo is curious to hear about how wives are best managed, and asks his father, who tells him they must be beaten, especially when they are as stubborn as Celie. Celie tries to make herself wooden, like a tree. This, she says, is how she knows that 'trees fear man'. Harpo tells Celie that he is in love with a girl. He has only winked at her in church, but he tells Celie that they plan to marry, although he is only seventeen, and she fifteen, and he has not yet spoken to her. This may be why he has asked his father's advice about wives.

bug round
yall you (plural)
Amen corner at prayer

LETTER 14   Shug Avery is coming to town

Shug Avery is coming to town to sing at the Lucky Star saloon. Celie and Mr — are very excited. Mr — dresses carefully, for once. Pink posters, picturing Shug as 'Queen Honeybee', are fastened to trees. Celie has no hope of attending a performance, but dreams of seeing Shug perform.

orkestra a blues band
hick country bumpkin
like Indian Chiefs covered with feathers
Queen Honeybee because she is sweet; 'Shug' is an abbreviation of Sugar

LETTER 15   Celie works while Mr — mopes

Mr — spends the weekend in town, returning tired and sad. Celie longs to question him about Shug. She works long hours in the field chopping cotton, unaided by Mr —, who makes a feeble attempt to help before returning to the verandah to smoke his pipe and stare into space.

Where you all children at ...? where are your and Shug's children ...?
Feel like snakes evil thoughts

LETTER 16   Mr — is still lovesick. Celie and Harpo do all the work

The lovesick Mr — now sits hopelessly all day, staring at nothing. Harpo, afraid of his father, is obliged to do all the ploughing. Wife and son labour like slaves. Celie thinks that Harpo's weakness makes him look womanly. Harpo is still in love.

LETTER 17   Sofia makes her presence felt

Harpo's girl's father rejects him as a suitor because his mother's murder is still reckoned a disgrace. Harpo suffers nightmares, reliving the scene of his mother's death. The 'boyfriend' shot her in the stomach and she died in Harpo's arms. Waking in the night, Harpo trembles and protests to Celie that his mother was not to blame.

Celie is kind to Mr —'s children, but has no affection, or any other feeling about them. Harpo continues to confide in her, however, praising the beauty of his girl, whom he now names as Sofia. He hopes that he will be regarded as a more acceptable husband once he has succeeded in making her pregnant. Once she is pregnant, he brings her to visit his father. They come marching up the road, hand in hand, Sofia in front. She is a large, strong girl, intelligent and independent, quite unafraid of Mr —. She has left home, but is living with her married sister; she tells Mr — that she will wait there until Harpo is allowed to marry her.

After Sofia's departure, the men are at a loss what to do or say, for once, because they are unaccustomed to such an outspoken woman.

chifferobe wardrobe
Bright having light-brown skin

LETTER 18   Harpo marries Sofia

Harpo marries Sofia; the baby in her arms is a big 'nursing' boy. He brings them back to a small house on his father's land, which they repair. Harpo begins to receive wages and he works more willingly. Sofia remains a strong, confident girl, and they are happy together. Only Mr — is cynical about their future.

goose encourage
mash crushed
switch the traces on you deceive you with another man

LETTER 19   Celie betrays Sofia

Trouble comes from Harpo's fixed idea that Sofia ought to obey him. She loves him, but has no intention of behaving like the submissive Celie. Mr — disapproves. Wives are like children, he says, and must be beaten if they are to be kept in order. Celie thinks that the marriage, now three years old, would be a happy one if Harpo would only forget his father's teaching and accept Sofia as she is. But Celie also resents Sofia's independent ways, and especially dislikes seeing Sofia pity her. When Harpo asks for advice, she tells him to beat Sofia. The next time she sees Harpo, his face is a mass of bruises. He tells unlikely tales about a mule and a barn door. Sofia retains the upper hand.

It is an especially clever detail to make Celie advise Harpo to beat Sofia. It is a lifelike moment of weakness (afterwards bitterly regretted) and true to the behaviour of oppressed people who sometimes do fall into the oppressor's ways of thinking.

primping preening, smartening up

LETTER 20   Sofia proves more than a match for Harpo

Harpo and Sofia continue to have fist-fights. Celie witnesses one appalling contest, where they tear their house apart, and which Sofia wins. She and Harpo, with the two babies, leave in the wagon the next day, as she wanted, to visit her married sister.

hants ghosts
ease on back out eased my way out

LETTER 21   Sofia proclaims that women must learn to fight

Celie has trouble getting to sleep for over a month and decides that she is suffering for her sin against Sofia. She hopes that Sofia will not find out that she advised Harpo to use violence. Harpo tells, however, and Sofia is furious. Celie confesses that she is jealous of Sofia's ability to fight for herself. Sofia talks about her childhood. She was one of twelve children, six girls and six boys. The girls were obliged to learn to fight, and to stick together. No girl is safe from her own male kin, Sofia says, unless she can fight. Celie says, piously, that life is short, but Heaven will be for ever. Sofia recommends bashing Mr —'s head open, and thinking about Heaven later.

They collapse in laughter, and then set to work on quilt-making. Celie can sleep once more.

For the rest of the novel, quilt-making is a symbol of women's solidarity (see Symbolism).

witch hazel a herbal remedy for ills
Bible say ... mother see Deuteronomy 5:16
Old Maker God

LETTER 22   **Shug falls sick. Albert brings her home**

Shug is ill, and everyone has turned against her, except Mr — and Celie. The preacher at church and her parents at home have condemned her, but Mr — goes off in his wagon and brings her home five days later, sick and stumbling, but still 'dressed to kill'. Celie is fascinated by the 'mean' look on Shug's now feverish face, and by the enigmatic tone of her cackling voice. Her greeting is 'mean': 'You sure *is* ugly'.

got his mouth on speaks against
amen all through the novel 'amen' tends to imply mindless religious conformism
mean American usage has the senses of 'hostile', 'malicious', 'troublesome' and 'hard to defeat'

LETTER 23   **Albert nurses Shug devotedly**

Shug is sicker than Celie's mother on her deathbed, but she is more 'evil', Celie says, and that keeps her alive. Her strength of will is undiminished. She hectors Mr —, whom she calls Albert, even forbidding him to smoke in her sickroom, where he mopes in the shadows. Celie is astonished to see how easily he can be subdued. She had forgotten his name. She notices for the first time that Albert has a weak chin. It is also the first time that he and she share a concern, in their common devotion to Shug. He consults Celie, for once, asking her if she minds having Shug in the house.

Although Celie continues to speak of Mr — until almost the end of the novel, the reader is likely to follow other characters in thinking of him as Albert. He seems less of a monster from now on. He sheds a tear of sympathy for Shug at the end of this letter.

LETTER 24   Celie bathes Shug and falls in love with her

Although Shug and Albert have had three children together, he is uncomfortable about giving her a bath, so Celie has to do it. When Shug is naked for her bath, Celie is so attracted by the sight of her long body that she wonders if she has turned into a man. Her hands tremble as she washes her patient. They begin to talk. Shug rejects Celie's deferential 'ma'am'. She tells Celie she never misses her children, who live with their grandmother.

Celie's powers of expression have been improving and this letter, where she discovers her own sexual nature, is full of examples of her growing fluency and her imaginative use of figurative language (see Textual Analysis).

bat her eyes flutter her eyelids

LETTER 25   Shug recovers

Shug refuses food, confining herself to coffee and cigarettes while she looks through fashion magazines, seeming to be puzzled by their images of white women in high society. Celie tempts her successfully with the smell of home-cured ham. This puts Celie and Albert in so good a humour that they laugh together. Albert looks slightly crazy because he has been so afraid.

The pictures in the magazine are an indication that we are now in the 1920s.

grits porridge made from ground oats
biscuit scones
flapjacks pancakes

LETTER 26   Shug composes a song for Celie

Shug begins to get better, tended by the attentive, loving Celie. She treats Shug with the care she would like to show her daughter Olivia. Shug composes a song inspired, she says, by Celie.

a rat to pomp a pad of hair to fluff out the wearer's own hair
scratch out my head draw from my mind

LETTER 27   **Albert's father is a most unwelcome visitor**

Albert's father arrives; a small, pompous and indignant man. While he denounces Shug, Celie spits in his glass of water and wonders how to prepare ground glass. Albert's brother Tobias is the next visitor. He brings a ridic-ulously small box of chocolates and a large amount of vulgar curiosity. Celie teaches Shug to sew quilts. Sitting between Shug and Albert, united with them in opposition to Tobias and all the outside world, she feels happy.

This letter incident brings Albert and Celie closer than ever before, in shared hostility to the old man and loyalty to Shug.

nappy fuzzy
a right smart a large part
cornrowed done in small plaits
fly speck very small

LETTER 28   **Harpo is overeating**

Sofia and Celie work on a quilt. Sofia is worried about Harpo, who has become absurdly gluttonous, consuming vast amounts of fattening food. Harpo likes housework and Sofia likes working outdoors, so they ought to get on well together, but Harpo is obviously unhappy about something. He gorges between meals, and, the women agree, has started to look pregnant. Celie watches him with growing concern.

You feeling yourself Sofia thinks Celie is talking nonsense
clabber curds
troth trough

LETTER 29   **Celie urges Harpo to accept Sofia's independent nature**

Harpo breaks down in tears one night when he is staying with Albert and Celie. He tells Celie how much he wants Sofia to obey him, or at least pay some attention to what he tells her. Sofia refuses to 'mind' him, and she blacks his eyes when he tries to beat her. Celie urges him to accept Sofia as she is, a good wife who loves him. Harpo seems unable to take this advice.

LETTER 30   Sofia intends to leave Harpo

Celie visits Sofia. It seems that Harpo is overeating because he hopes to match his wife's weight and improve his chances in their up to now unequal combats. But Sofia is weary of Harpo's obsession with power: he wants a dog, not a wife, she says. She intends to take the children and move to her sister's home. Celie is shocked, but also filled with envy at the idea of having such a refuge. Sofia still loves her husband but their sexual relations are now cold and unfulfilling. All that she really wants is a change of scene for a while.

shingles thin oblong pieces of roofing material

like running ... on itself her love for another woman seems to lead nowhere

LETTER 31   Sofia leaves Harpo

Sofia's sisters arrive in strength to escort her. Celie presents her with the finished quilt. Powerless to stop his wife's departure, Harpo is a sorry sight as he says goodbye to his children, changing the baby for the last time and drying his tears on the nappy.

seining netting

Dilsey, Coco and Boo the names of their cows

LETTER 32   Harpo opens a jukejoint

Six months have passed since Sofia left. Harpo is greatly changed. Having been thoroughly domesticated as a husband, he is now determined to make money and is converting his house into a jukejoint where his friend Swain will play jazz and people will come out from town for dancing and entertainment. He seems sure Sofia will not return.

jukejoint a bar and dance-hall; it had to be out of easy reach of the police because of Prohibition, the law banning the sale of alcohol in the United States, in force 1920–33

LETTER 33   Shug sings 'Miss Celie's song' at the jukejoint

In the first few weeks nobody comes to Harpo's jukejoint, apart from friendly visits by Albert and Shug. Then Harpo recruits Shug as a singer. Posters go back on the trees. The bar is filled to overcrowding on Saturday nights. Celie is not allowed to go to such a low establishment; she longs in vain to hear Shug sing. Then Albert's objections are overruled by Shug herself, and Celie goes to a performance. She is jealous because Shug seems to have eyes only for Albert. Then Shug sings 'Miss Celie's song', the one Celie helped her to compose.

'Miss Celie's song' is a love song, a symbol of the bond that now unites Shug and Celie. Shug's formal 'Miss' is itself a mark of her respect and love. Celie has never been so highly regarded or so happy.

The mention of Bessie Smith, Empress of the Blues, is a further reminder of the cultural background of the 1920s.

box guitar

chitlins chitterlings, fried pork intestines

shifts dresses

Bessie Smith (1894–1937) a brilliant entertainer and singer; known as 'the Empress of the Blues', she was immensely successful in the 1920s. The American dramatist Edward Albee (b.1928) based his play, *The Death of Bessie Smith* (1960), on the (groundless) popular belief that her life might have been saved after her fatal motor accident if a hospital for whites had admitted her

sassy cheeky

LETTER 34   Shug and Harpo are in business together

Shug sings every weekend at Harpo's place and they both make good money. Singing restores Shug to full health and she decides to leave. When she hears Celie's fear that Albert will start beating her again once she has gone, she promises to stay until she can be sure that he will not do it.

lightening bugs fireflies

LETTER 35   Shug makes Celie jealous by sleeping with Albert

Celie is jealous because Shug is now sleeping with Albert. When she discusses this with Shug, she conceals the fact that it is Shug, not Albert, she wants to keep for herself. Shug tries to explain her passion for Albert: he is small and amusing and 'smells right'. She is amazed by Celie's confession that she has never enjoyed sexual relations with men. She tells

LETTER 35 continued

Celie this means she is still a virgin, and begins to teach her about sexual pleasure. Celie still feels jealous at night.

rassle rustle

not with my sponge and all refers to her method of contraception

LETTER 36   Trouble at the jukejoint

Sofia returns. She appears at the jukejoint with Henry Broadnax, known as Buster, a man who looks like a prize-fighter. Sofia and Harpo dance, until Harpo's girlfriend, known as Squeak, quarrels with, and slaps, Sofia. Sofia's tough upbringing has made her return any blow by instinct. She knocks Squeak down, dislodging two teeth.

white lightening corn whiskey

scandless scandal

teenouncy cheeky

LETTER 37   Sofia is in prison after striking the mayor

Celie advises Squeak to make Harpo call her by her real name, Mary Agnes, because that will make him take her seriously when he is in trouble. Trouble has come: Sofia is in prison. Celie relates to Mary Agnes how Sofia met Miss Millie, the mayor's wife, who made a fuss of her children and then asked if Sofia would care to work as her maid. Appalled at the thought of becoming a white woman's servant, Sophia replied, 'Hell, no'. The mayor slapped Sofia, who knocked him down. Celie cannot go on with the story, so Albert tells how the police beat Sofia before they arrested her, their guns on Buster, the prize-fighter. Mary Agnes runs to comfort Harpo. Albert persuades the sheriff to allow a prison visit.

Sofia is badly injured and bruised purple all over. Celie attends to her as well as she can.

> We are reminded that this era of glorious black music was also one of cruel injustice for many African Americans. This letter marks a turning point in the plot, and begins the section of the novel concerned with Sofia's sufferings and endurance as a victim of injustice.

going on over colored making a fuss over black people

Just long ... colored so long as Albert remembers the difference in status between the white sheriff and himself
eggplant aubergine, coloured purple

LETTER 38   Sofia begins a twelve-year sentence

The prison visits take place twice a month for half an hour. Sofia works in the prison laundry, in horrible conditions. She learns to behave like Celie, always obedient. But the twelve years of her sentence are 'a long time to be good', as she ruefully jokes. Mary Agnes is helping Sofia's sister Odessa to look after the children.

LETTER 39   Sofia's friends take counsel

Celie, Shug, Mary Agnes, Odessa and two more of Sofia's sisters, Albert and the prize-fighter meet to discuss what to do, because they fear for Sofia's sanity. Harpo and the prize-fighter dream of violent action. Celie dreams of rescue by angels. A practical plan is devised when it is realised that the light-skinned Mary Agnes is related to the white prison-warden, Bubber Hodges. Bubber is her uncle.

This letter makes the ironical point that 'black' and 'white' people, social worlds apart on grounds of 'colour', were often closely related.

LETTER 40   Mary Agnes visits the prison warden

Mary Agnes is dressed as a white woman, except that the clothes are patchier. The plan is for her to remind the warden that they are related and that he once gave her a present when she was a child. She must then persuade him that Sofia is quite happy in the laundry, but would loathe being forced to work as a white woman's maid: that would be a real punishment. The idea behind the plan is that the warden will believe that Mary Agnes wishes Sofia harm as she lives with Harpo, and as her kinsman he will fulfil her wish and make Sofia a maid.

look like a quilt having a chequered design
Uncle Tom *Uncle Tom's Cabin* (1851–2), by Harriet Elizabeth Beecher Stowe (1811–96), is a novel depicting the miseries of slavery in America. Uncle Tom gave his name to the type of black person who was deferential to whites

LETTER 41   The warden commits 'a little fornication'

The warden is not pleased to be reminded of his kinship with Squeak. He listens to her story, and then asks her to undo her clothing and commits what he calls 'a little fornication'. She goes home with her dress torn. She has suffered in a good cause, however, and has acquired a new self-confidence, in spite of humiliation. When Harpo says he loves her, she demands her rightful name, not Squeak but Mary Agnes.

crackers an insulting term
or just my color her light skin

LETTER 42   Mary Agnes becomes a singer

Six months pass, and Mary Agnes becomes a singer. Her small, high voice seems odd after Shug's singing, but she soon becomes popular. She is still angry about the teeth that were knocked out, but she helps to care for Sofia's children all the same.

LETTER 43   Sofia is a nursemaid for Miss Millie's children

Three years later, the prison authorities have followed Mary Agnes's suggestion and transferred Sofia from the laundry to duties outside the prison as nursemaid to Miss Millie's children. The mayor's six-year-old son shouts orders, and tries to kick Sofia. She moves out of the way, and the boy hurts his foot. Sofia would be blamed if it were not for the little girl, Eleanor Jane, who dotes on her nurse and testifies to what really happened. Sofia has recovered her physical health, but she broods on violent revenge.

LETTER 44   Sofia sees her own children for fifteen minutes

The mayor has bought his wife a new car, but he declines to teach her to drive. Sofia, who used to drive Buster's car, gives Miss Millie lessons. In return, Miss Millie drives Sofia home to spend Christmas Day with her family. She is a well-meaning but ineffectual woman, who does not let Sofia sit beside her in the car because that is not done 'in the South'. As things turn out, Millie's incompetence spoils Sofia's one holiday, and she manages to spend only fifteen minutes with her family.

LETTER 45   Celie is jealous because Shug has married

The story of Celie and Shug is resumed; we can work out later that several
years must have passed since the last letter. Shug comes to stay for
Christmas and brings a surprise – a new husband. He is a toothy, vulgar
man called Grady whom Celie instantly dislikes. She and Albert are
extremely jealous. Rich and famous, Shug is driving a new car. She is slow
to greet Celie, but does so warmly.

LETTER 46   An unhappy Christmas

The men drink their way through Christmas, while the women work, talk
and celebrate. Shug seems indifferent to the pain she is causing Albert and
Celie. Celie confesses that she still is, in Shug's sense, a virgin.

> **Sophie Tucker** (1884–1966) black American singer, actress and entertainer.
> Known as 'the Last of the Red Hot Mommas', she sang with great attack, but
> also had sentimental songs, including 'The Lady is a Tramp'
> **Duke Ellington** Edward Kennedy 'Duke' Ellington (1899–1974), black
> American band leader; the most influential writer and arranger in the history
> of jazz. His compositions include 'Mood Indigo'

LETTER 47   Shug sleeps with Celie, who relates her early sufferings

Albert and Grady go off in the car and Shug sleeps with Celie for warmth.
Celie tells her how she was raped by Alphonso when she was fourteen, and
she recalls the horror of those days as she lies in Shug's arms. They make
love.

LETTER 48   Shug encourages Mary Agnes to start a singing career

Sleeping with Shug feels like heaven to Celie. It lasts until the men return
at dawn, when Albert falls into bed, drunk and snoring. Grady annoys Shug
by calling her Mama, and by making eyes at Mary Agnes. Shug is generous
to her, however, and encourages her to start a career as a professional singer.

> **like somebody from the North** attempting to appear sophisticated

LETTER 49   A letter from Nettie

Celie has a letter from Nettie at long last. Celie has told Shug about the
mystery of Nettie's failure to write. Shug has seen Albert pocketing letters
with foreign stamps. We can guess why Nettie's letters have never reached
Celie. Nettie's letter shows that she has guessed too: Albert must have been
intercepting her letters. She continues to write at Christmas and Easter,
just in case one may get through. She says that Celie's son and Olivia are
alive and well and coming home soon.

> Another major turning point in the story is reached here. From now
> on, groups of Nettie's letters alternate with Celie's, and so, therefore,
> does the narrative **point of view**. The African part of the story
> henceforth counterpoints the American (see Theme on Slavery, and
> Text 2 of Textual Analysis).

> **mailbox** on a post by the road, well away from the house
> **a little fat white woman** the Queen of England, we learn in the next letter,
> although the King's head would have appeared on British stamps at any date
> during the period covered by the novel

LETTER 50   Shug relates her early life

Shug has become friendly with Albert again. She walks to the mailbox with
him. This is how she secured Nettie's letter. Celie is so angry about Albert's
theft that she is in danger of cutting his throat until Shug takes the razor
from her. Shug tells Celie about her early life. Her puritanical mother soon
rejected her. She found comfort in loving Albert, who joked and danced
better than anyone when he was young. Shug bore his three children.
When she was finally turned out of the house by her parents, she went to
live with a 'wild' aunt in Memphis, Tennessee. Albert married Annie Julia
because his father insisted that Shug was 'trash' and Albert was too weak to
stand up for himself. Shug regrets her heartless behaviour to Annie Julia.
She is puzzled by Albert's cruelty to Celie.

> **reefer** of cannabis
> **Lillie** the first mention of her Christian name
> **the moochie** the partners in this slow dance stand very close

LETTER 51   A cache of Nettie's letters is found

Celie and Shug find bundles of letters from Nettie in Albert's trunk. They steam the envelopes open and reclaim the contents, replacing the empty envelopes in the trunk.

LETTER 52   Nettie's letter from years ago urges Celie to leave Albert. She is staying with the clergyman who adopted Celie's child

In this letter from Nettie to Celie, Nettie urges Celie to leave Albert. She relates how Albert followed and tried to rape her on the day she fled from his house. She fought him off. In fury he threatened that neither sister would ever hear from the other again. Nettie has reached the Reverend Mr —'s house, and found Olivia there.

> Nettie's letters take us back in time. This letter must have been written soon after Nettie ran away. As the novel progresses, Nettie's letters become gradually more recent, until the sisters are united in time as well as place at the close (see Dating Events).

LETTER 53   Nettie helps Samuel and Corrine in their church work, and lives as a member of the family. Olivia has a brother, Adam

From Nettie to Celie, a few weeks later – Nettie begs for a letter as soon as possible. The woman Celie met in the store is called Corrine and her husband is called Samuel. The little girl is now known as Olivia. There is also a little boy called Adam. The family are kind to Nettie, involving her in their work for the church.

> We learn that Adam is Celie's son in the letter after next. The significance of his name appears in Letter 87.

sanctified religious dedicated Christians

LETTER 54   Samuel and Corrine are to go to Africa as missionaries

From Nettie to Celie – Nettie is very worried about Celie's failure to reply and about her own situation. She is unable to find suitable work. Corrine and Samuel are about to go to Africa as missionaries. She begs for a letter.

LETTER 55   **Nettie is in Africa. She means to write regular letters to Celie even though there is no reply**

From Nettie to Celie – Celie's headnote to this letter tells us that it is dated two months after Letter 54. Nettie is now in Africa. She wrote almost every day of the journey, but destroyed these letters in a moment of despair. Now she has decided to write to Celie in the same desperate hope that made Celie start writing to God. She describes a meeting she had before leaving with a woman who we know from her description must be Sofia (at the time she worked as Miss Millie's nursemaid). She then hears from Samuel and Corrine about how this lady came to be imprisoned. This episode inspired her to accept Samuel's invitation to accompany the family to 'the middle of Africa' as a missionary. She assures Celie that Olivia and Adam are her children and that they are growing up happily.

> Unusually, a reference is made to the date of this letter: 'dated two months later'. That implies that the earlier letters were dated within a shorter space of time. At the time this letter was written, less than a year can have passed since Celie and Nettie parted (see Dating Events).

Atlanta the state capital of Georgia
Milledgeville a town in Georgia

LETTER 56   **Nettie visits Harlem and admires the dignity of its residents**

From Nettie to Celie – Nettie feels one of the family rather than a maid; she studies and she teaches the children. She describes her stay in New York before boarding the ship, and praises Harlem, where black people live with dignity and faith. The enthusiastic support and generous fund-raising of church people in Harlem is contrasted with the cold and haughty manners of white people in the Missionary Society.

gored formed with wedge-shaped panels of cloth
boater a flat straw-hat
Harlem the section of New York City between East River and Harlem River at the northern end of Manhattan Island
Speke John Hanning Speke (1827–64), British explorer. He found and named

Lake Victoria [Victoria Nyanza], and explored the upper waters of the Nile
Livingstone the Reverend Dr David Livingstone (1813–73), British missionary
and explorer
Stanley Sir Henry Morton Stanley (1841–1904), British explorer and
journalist. He was foreign correspondent for the *New York Herald* when he met
Livingstone, then exploring the sources of the Nile, and greeted him 'Doctor
Livingstone, I presume?', at Ujiji, on Lake Tanganyika, in 1871

LETTER 57   Nettie describes the voyage to Africa

From Nettie to Celie – Nettie praises Samuel's wisdom and kindness. She
is enthusiastic about the ship on which they crossed the Atlantic, and about
the strange ways of England, where some fund-raising was done. She is
beginning to learn about the colonial history of Africa. She has discovered
that slaves transported to America were often bought from within the
slave-trade practised by Africans. The journey from England is via Lisbon,
Dakar and Monrovia.

J.A. Rogers Joel Augustus Rogers (1883–1966), historian and journalist. His
From Superman to Man was published in 1917. His controversial views on
African history met with opposition
vesper service evening church service

LETTER 58   Nettie visits Senegal and Liberia

From Nettie to Celie – she recounts more about the journey, including the
stop in Senegal, then a French colony, and the visit to Monrovia. Nettie
finds that there are many white men in Africa, and that not all are
missionaries. The president of the African-governed state of Liberia seems
remote from the problems of his people. Nettie hears the singing of
exhausted workers in the cacao fields and learns that the plantations are
Dutch-owned. She ends by describing the intense emotion of homecoming
when she, Corrine and Samuel first saw the coast of Africa and gave thanks
to God.

Senegalese Wolof and Fulani are spoken in Senegal
Tubman this must be a predecessor of the noted President (William V.S.)
Tubman (1895–1971), who took office in 1944
cacao the cacao tree; its seeds are used to make cocoa and chocolate

LETTER 59   Shug comforts Celie

Celie resumes her letters to God. When Shug pleads with her not to murder Albert, on the grounds that his removal would leave her only Grady to sleep with, Celie begs Shug to sleep with her in future, and Shug agrees.

Thou Shalt Not Kill see Matthew 19:18

LETTER 60   Celie starts her pants-making career

Celie and Shug sleep together 'like sisters' because Celie is too angry, at the thought of the letterless years, to make love. Shug persuades her to sew herself some pants; her dress is unsuitable for work in the fields, and pants will suit her.

pants trousers (U.S.)

LETTER 61   Celie frets about her children's parentage

Celie is looking forward to Nettie's return, but is beginning to worry about her children, fearing that their conception (which she believes to have been incestuous), may have injured their development. She quotes within this letter to God an entire letter from Nettie.

Nettie describes how they left the ship at a small port somewhere in West Africa and were led to the village where they are to work. The land of Olinka is described. The people are amazed by the sight of the women missionaries, and they gather round Nettie and Corrine, touching their dresses and hair. Their guide, Joseph, explains that the missionaries who have come before were all white, and furthermore, only men have come this far. The Olinka ask questions, and one comments that the two children resemble Nettie, not Corrine. The Olinka are healthy but very poor by American standards. They harvest enough yams, cassava and other produce to keep them self-sufficient. They count themselves rich in roofleaf which is both the covering for their huts and their 'god' (they worship the leaf as a symbol of divine protection).

Mention here of roofleaf's significance in Olinka religion prepares for the catastrophe in Letter 80, pp. 192–3, when tin is provided for the roofs of workers' huts. Nettie's sympathy with African religion develops in the course of her letters (except when it is an obstacle to women's emancipation), as she witnesses colonial disregard for traditional beliefs and as her own faith becomes less doctrinaire (see Text 2 of Textual Analysis).

dunces she fears they may be mentally handicapped

pidgin English a trade-language drawing grammar and vocabulary from English and other sources; it often serves as a medium between speakers of different West African languages

bush forest or uncultivated countryside

palm wine made from fermented palm sap

cassava ... yam plants with starchy tubers

millet a type of food grain

LETTER 62   Nettie faces difficulties in her work. Corrine is beginning to be jealous

From Nettie to Celie – Nettie seldom has time to put pen to paper, but whatever she is doing, she is writing to Celie in her mind. She writes realistically about West African insect bites and other difficulties of settling in, including cultural differences. Olivia is the only girl in the village school because the Olinka believe that education should be for boys alone. Olivia compares this narrow-mindedness with that of 'white people at home who don't want colored people to learn'. She hopes that she and her Olinka friend Tashi will grow up to have more interesting lives than women are allowed in the village. Corrine is becoming jealous of Nettie as a rival. Domestic troubles seem to be in store.

Schweitzer Dr Albert Schweitzer (1875–1965), German theologian, philosopher and musician, who abandoned a brilliant career in 1913, to run a mission-hospital at Lambaréné (in present-day Gabon)

LETTER 63   Olivia's friend Tashi learns Western ways

From Nettie to Celie – Tashi's parents complain that Olivia's influence is distancing their daughter from the life and customs of the Olinka people. Nettie tells Tashi's father that Africa is changing and will soon be more than just a man's world. He defends the dignity of Olinka women; superior, he says, to the condition of an outcast and drudge such as Nettie. He says he is willing to receive Olivia in his house, where she will be able to learn true womanly ways.

LETTER 64 Nettie thinks about her life in Africa

From Nettie to Celie – five years more have passed. A road is being built through the forest. The Olinka welcome the road-builders with gifts and friendship. Corrine is growing more jealous of Nettie, and has asked her not to invite Samuel to her hut. Nettie now values the company of her niece and nephew more than ever. Tashi has lost her father, who died of malaria. Nettie broods about the lives of Olinka women, who seem happy although they have to share husbands and cannot have men as friends. She thinks the women spoil their husbands and that this makes the men 'childish'. She also notes that Olinka men have the power of life and death over their women.

> **Uncle Remus** Joel Chandler Harris (1848–1908) published *Uncle Remus, his Songs and Sayings* in 1881, and the classic series of *Uncle Remus* books followed. An old black American tells stories to a small boy. Among the animal characters drawn from black folk-tales are Brer (Brother) Rabbit and Brer Fox. Like Alice Walker, he was born in Eatonton, Georgia
> **keening** lamentation for the dead

LETTER 65 Colonial rule brings many difficulties

From Nettie to Celie – another year has passed. The road the Olinka welcomed has flattened most of their village. The whole region, furthermore, has been bought by a British company and the forests are being cleared for rubber plantations. The chief's appeal to the governor only resulted in a demand for taxes. Essential village buildings, including the school, have been rebuilt, however; several girls now attend the school. Corrine has been ill.

LETTER 66 Corrine's jealousy increases. Rubber plantations ruin the Olinka hunting grounds

From Nettie to Celie – times are becoming ever more difficult. Corrine frets because the children resemble Nettie. She demands that Nettie and Samuel swear on the Bible that they never had an affair. The fields and hunting grounds of the Olinka have been destroyed to make space for planting rubber.

LETTER 67   **Nettie has learnt from Samuel that she and Celie are not Alphonso's children**

From Nettie to Celie – Samuel has always thought that the children must be Nettie's. That is why he first took her in and later invited her to go to Africa. Samuel turns out to possess crucial information about the sisters' background. When he was a young man, he used to be acquainted with Alphonso. He is sure that Nettie and Celie are the children not of Alphonso but of a trader lynched by white rivals. Alphonso married this man's widow, who was afflicted by mental illness. This woman must be Celie and Nettie's mother and Alphonso their stepfather. Nettie prays that this letter may reach Celie with the wonderful news that 'Pa is not our pa!'

LETTER 68   **Celie is amazed and delighted**

This brief note is Celie's last letter to God until Letter 90. It records her amazed and delighted discovery that her children were not incestuously conceived, and that all her assumptions about family have been turned upside down. Shug is going to take her away, to Tennessee. She ends by telling God that he must be asleep, to have kept all this from her.

LETTER 69   **Alphonso confirms that he is not the sisters' father**

From Celie to Nettie – Celie visits Alphonso. She and Shug drive there in the Packard, wearing their new 'flower pants' as emblems of liberation. There are real flowers everywhere about them as they drive through the countryside on the new tarmac roads. Alphonso seems to be enjoying great prosperity; he has a new, fifteen-year-old wife. He has a white man working in his store. He says that he kept the true story of Celie's parentage secret because it was too sad to tell to little girls. Shug and Celie look for but cannot find the graves of Celie's parents.

bought me my own white boy hired a white man as an assistant; Alphonso characteristically employs the language of slavery

cockleburrs prickly plants

LETTER 70   Corrine is dying

From Nettie to Celie – Corrine is dying. Nettie has told her about the children's parentage, but she cannot believe it, or remember the meeting with Celie in the store (in Letter 10).

LETTER 71   Corrine dies, acknowledging that Nettie has told the truth about the past

From Nettie to Celie – Nettie has tried to make Corrine remember. She has found in Corrine's trunk the quilt she made from the cloth she bought the day she met Celie; this revives a memory long suppressed, as Corrine now admits, because Celie was so like Olivia. She recalls the incident with the white storekeeper that Celie writes of in Letter 10. Corrine dies just after acknowledging that Nettie has told the truth.

Corrine's deathbed reconciliation and her convenient removal from the story to allow for Nettie's marriage to Samuel are reminiscent of conventions of **closure** in Victorian fiction, and in popular entertainment today.

hitching post to tie horses
appliquéd in needlework, pieces of one material applied to the surface of another
Spelman Seminary see About the Author in Background

LETTER 72   Corrine is buried

From Nettie to Celie – Corrine is given a traditional Olinka funeral. Samuel and the children feel their loss keenly. Nettie dreams of seeing Celie again. Two ill-mannered white men have been to survey the village. Nettie has told Samuel about her letter-writing.

Female genital mutilation, a topic alluded to in this letter, is a major theme in Alice Walker's novel *Possessing the Secret of Joy* (1992), where Adam and Tashi appear as characters (see Other Works by Alice Walker).

my friend menstrual period
one ritual circumcision
faces painted white the colour of death and mourning in many parts of Africa

LETTER 73   Celie and Shug talk about God

From Celie to Nettie – Celie has stopped writing to God because, she says, 'if he ever listened to poor colored women the world would be a different place'. In spite of her reputation as 'a devil', Shug dissuades Celie from blasphemy. They discuss religion. Celie admits that her idea of God was a mental picture of an old grey-bearded white man. Shug tells her that God is not a person outside her but a power within. God can be seen in the beauty of nature. He can even be known through sexual pleasure, 'some of the best stuff God did'. Shug believes that God wants to be admired. She says, 'it pisses God off' if people pass a field of purple without noticing. Above all the idea of God as male has to be abandoned. That falsifies one's views of everything.

In this letter Shug expounds Alice Walker's own views on religion (see *The Same River Twice*, pp. 42–3, for example). Nettie confesses in Letter 86 that her faith has become less doctrinaire (see Theme on Religious Belief).

LETTER 74   Celie is to leave Albert. Women are taking charge

From Celie to Nettie – Celie relates the story of Sofia, who is out of prison and restored to her family, although now almost a stranger to her children. Shug and Celie announce that they are going to Memphis, Tennessee. Celie denounces Albert for robbing her of Nettie: she is leaving him to 'enter the Creation'. Mary Agnes is leaving Harpo to go north as a singer. Sofia is called back to look after the mayor's family, but undertakes on her return to look after Harpo and his child by Mary Agnes, named Jolentha but known as Suzie Q. The women have taken charge.

dime   a coin worth ten cents
bangs   fringes of hair

LETTER 75   Hard words between Albert and Celie

From Celie to Nettie – Shug, Celie, Mary Agnes and Grady are travelling to Memphis. Grady is now infatuated with Mary Agnes. Albert reacts badly to Celie's departure, heaping insults on her. In return she curses him: she threatens that everything will turn out badly for him until he recognises his crimes and decides to treat her properly.

This letter contains one of the most powerful dramatic scenes in the novel (see Text 3 of Textual Analysis).

LETTER 76   Celie and Shug set up house together

From Celie to Nettie – Shug owns a big house in Memphis, decorated throughout with figures and designs of elephants and turtles. The friends cook and listen to music. The newspapers show them how badly the world is being managed. Celie becomes obsessed with making pants. A few can be made for tolerable men, such as Odessa's husband Jack. Shug encourages her to start a business, selling brightly coloured pants to women everywhere.

collards leaves of a cabbage-like vegetable
souse pigs' trotters and other parts, pickled
betsy bugs small insects
Unlimited a play on 'Limited Company'

LETTER 77   Celie runs 'Folkspants, Unlimited'

From Celie to Nettie – Celie now has all she desires except the safe return of Nettie and the children. Her firm, 'Folkspants, Unlimited', is prospering. She has two assistants, twins called Jerene and Darlene. Darlene is trying to teach her correct English. She tries to make Celie say 'we' rather than 'us' when Celie says 'us not so hot'. Celie is planning a pair of pants for Sofia with one leg red and the other purple.

LETTER 78   Sofia buries her mother, and learns to smoke reefers

From Celie to Nettie – Sofia's mother has died. Although pall-bearers at funerals have always been men, Sofia fights a successful battle against male prejudice, and she and her sisters carry the coffin to the grave. Celie is now much altered by Shug's influence: she teaches Harpo and Sofia how to smoke 'reefer'. Celie says that she takes the drug when she wants to talk to God or to make love. Sofia is shocked. They sit round the kitchen table and smoke reefers until they hear a mysterious humming, which may, perhaps, be the murmur of the universe.

fight the good fight from the hymn, 'Fight the good fight/With all thy might', by Fr. J.S.B. Monsell (1811–75)

LETTER 79   Albert learns to do housework

From Celie to Nettie – Albert has reformed. He is now clean and hardworking, and even does housework and cooking. It seems that he deteriorated rapidly after Celie left him. He was rescued, however, by Harpo, who showed him great kindness. Harpo also made him return all Celie's remaining letters from Nettie, so lifting the effect of her curse.

yall must still be dope you must still all be doped

cut my own switch prepare my own punishment

LETTER 80   Nettie and Samuel marry in England

From Nettie to Celie – Nettie is plump and grey-haired, and is now married to Samuel. The Olinka have been forced from their village by the rubber planters, and have to settle on a barren strip of land with no water supply for six months of the year. They suffer further indignity when they are reduced to buying tin to replace the sacred roofleaf. It is no surprise that they have lost whatever faith they may have had in missionaries. Nettie, Samuel and the children travel to England to seek help for the Olinka. On the journey, they meet the English lady who had been working as a missionary when they first arrived years before. She is returning to England to retire as she is now sixty-five, and she speaks of her early life in English upper-class society and how she sought escape from married life in England in missionary work. On arrival in England, Samuel and Nettie attend a meeting with a bishop whose only concern is the relationship between them now that Corrine is dead. He does not even consider the plight of the Olinka. Afterwards, Samuel talks of his doubts about their work, and reminisces about his early life with Corrine. He breaks down in tears, and in comforting him, Nettie reveals her love for him. They are married soon afterwards. Olivia reveals that Adam is unhappy in England because he misses Tashi. He is worried about her, as, in a gesture of support for traditional Olinka customs, she intends to undergo ritual facial scarring and circumcision. It seems clear that Adam loves Tashi.

Reference to 'a big war' is one of the hints to the novel's time-scheme. The year seems to be 1938 or 1939 (see Dating Events).

bloody cutting circumcision

the Belgian Congo the colonial name for the Democratic Republic of Congo.

See the note on King Leopold, below

Edward du Boyce W(illiam) E(dward) B(urghardt) Du Bois (pronounced Du Boyce) (*c.*1868–1963), scholar, poet and Pan-Africanist. He was the first black American to obtain a Harvard doctorate

King Leopold Leopold II (1835–1909), King of the Belgians (1865–1909); recognised in 1885 as sovereign of the Congo Free State, annexed as the Belgian Congo in 1908

LETTER 81   Nettie's family return to Africa

From Nettie to Celie – Nettie and Samuel have returned from England to Olinka. Tashi has undergone the traditional initiation ceremonies, but has become ashamed of the marks on her face. Adam refuses to speak to her. He is desperate to return to America.

LETTER 82   Alphonso has died

From Celie to Nettie – Alphonso's wife calls Celie to tell her that he is dead. The house and the business he ran were in fact owned by Celie's father, so they now belong to Celie and Nettie. Celie and Shug go to look at the house, and when they get there Celie finds Alphonso's tombstone which declares him to have been kind to the poor and helpless. Celie cannot believe that the beautiful house they find now belongs to her.

LETTER 83   Shug finds a boyfriend

From Celie to Nettie – Celie is broken-hearted because Shug has fallen in love with a young man called Germaine. Celie had spent the summer in Memphis working on the house she inherited in preparation for Nettie's arrival. When she returns, Shug talks eagerly about this nineteen-year-old, who plays the flute in her band, until Celie's evident grief checks her enthusiasm. She pleads for six months' grace: the affair cannot last longer than that. Celie grieves jealously nonetheless. Grady and Mary Agnes are growing marijuana in Panama.

fortune cookies they have 'fortunes' written on thin slips of paper inserted before baking
flittish name fancy name
boocoos (*French*) correctly, *beaucoup*, a lot

LETTER 84   Celie is resentful about Shug's young man. She and
             Albert begin to be friends

From Celie to Nettie – Sofia's youngest child (not Harpo's), Henrietta, is
very ill. Caring for her helps to keep Celie from despair at Shug's infidelity.
A diet of yams is prescribed, following African custom advocated by Nettie
in a letter, but the child cannot stand the taste, so it has to be cunningly
disguised. Celie and Albert draw closer together; talking about Shug is a
bond between them. Albert proposes that they resume married life, but
Celie speaks frankly, at last, of her physical repugnance at the sight of
naked men.

LETTER 85   A telegram informs Celie that Nettie is dead

From Celie to Nettie – an official telegram reports that Nettie and family
are believed drowned after the ship bringing them from Africa was sunk by
German mines. All Celie's letters to Nettie have, at the same time, been
returned unopened.

The false telegraph shows the incompetence of people in authority. It
also creates suspense in preparation for the happy ending in store.

LETTER 86   Nettie hopes to return to America

From Nettie to Celie – Tashi and her mother have run away to join a group
of rebels against white rule, known as mbeles. The Olinka are falling sick
because the destruction of their yam crops has removed their resistance to
malaria. Nettie is full of worries and hopes about returning to America. She
fears that Celie may be living in wretched conditions. She expects that life
will be hard for her own family once they are back in the United States. But
there will be much to discuss, says Nettie, always a teacher, including her
evolving conception of God. Africa has taught her to think of God as a
Spirit unconstrained by the images of one religion or another, to be seen in
Christ or in roofleaf. The letter ends with the dramatic news that Adam has
gone away in search of Tashi.

The reference to thirty years having passed since the sisters were last
together is another useful clue to the time-scheme. The date seems to
be 1940 or 1941 (see Dating Events).

To Be or Not to Be see *Hamlet*, Act III, Scene 1, line 55

LETTER 87   Love of Shug acts as a bond between Celie and Albert

Celie to Nettie – Celie stands naked before her mirror, contemplating the changes brought by the years, because she is afraid that Shug no longer loves her. Shug and Germaine are touring the country. Albert, although still known to Celie only as Mr —, is now her only friend at hand. She finds that in spite of all the wrongs he has done her she cannot hate him. He has reformed, and he too loves Shug. He protects Celie from the unwanted attentions of men Sofia and Harpo put in her way. Celie and Albert sit and reminisce, about earlier events in their lives together.

Sofia still has troubles. Miss Eleanor Jane, the mayor's daughter brought up by Sofia, is still devoted to her. Eleanor Jane keeps visiting Sofia, bringing her husband and baby and demanding admiration. Sofia would prefer to be left alone. After her sufferings she cannot accept this white woman as a friend, and she is too honest to pretend to feel warmth towards the baby. Other black women pretend, she tells Eleanor Jane, because they are afraid of whites.

Shug writes, describing her travels. Celie is angry with her, but tries to accept Shug's right to her own life. She and Albert talk about Shug. Albert says she is 'manly', but Celie thinks that her virtues are womanly. They also talk about pants, symbolic, they agree, of freedom and power in modern America. Celie tells him how men wear robes in Africa. Civilisation there is profoundly different in other ways. Africans believe that the first man was black and created long before Adam. The Olinka, she has heard from Nettie, worship the snake. Albert finds her good company.

the trees with you God on your side (since Shug has taught her that God is present in nature)

cotton gin a machine to separate seeds and other impurities from cotton; a symbol of white oppression of black people

adobe Shug describes a house made of sun-dried brick of clay and straw

a scanless scandalously

Omatangu the first man, in African myth

LETTER 88   Adam marries Tashi. The family leave Africa

From Nettie to Celie – Adam has brought Tashi home, protesting, from the rebels' camp. He caught up with and accompanied her and her mother to the mbeles' encampment. He persuaded them to return with him. Tashi is afraid to marry Adam because she thinks Americans will despise her. But Adam has his face marked with carvings like hers: he has become Adam Omatangu, Adam of Africa. Samuel then marries Adam and Tashi, and the whole family set out for the coast to find a ship bound for home.

LETTER 89   **Celie has Shug at home with her and dreams that Nettie may still be alive**

From Celie to Nettie – Shug has been trying to get news of Nettie from the State Department, but the men there are racialists and uncooperative. Celie has not lost hope that Nettie may be alive. Sofia is working in the store Celie and Nettie have inherited. She scares the white man hired in Alphonso's time. Eleanor Jane is caring for Henrietta. She has at long last found out the circumstances in which Sofia went to work for her family. Sofia thinks there is hope for Eleanor Jane yet. Albert sits on his verandah, sewing. He is designing a shirt to match Celie's pants. Shug's return home makes Celie happy, for the moment. Shug explains that Germaine has been sent away to college. Celie tells her that she has been spending time with Albert, mentioning him by name for the first time.

LETTER 90   **Happy ending**

'Dear God ... Dear Everything', Celie writes. Nettie and the children are home, to the happiest of reunions. Even Albert is included, as he counts now as 'family'. Mary Agnes has left Grady, and returned from Panama to look after Suzie Q. Tashi and Adam are admired by all. Celie knows that the young people think that she and her friends are old, but she thinks 'this the youngest us ever felt'.

PART THREE

CRITICAL APPROACHES

CHARACTERISATION

Alice Walker thinks of her characters as people. Creative writing for her is a process of discovery rather than invention. Her brief afterword says 'I thank everyone in this book for coming', and she has described the experience of waiting for her characters to make themselves known to her (see *In Search of Our Mothers' Gardens*, pp. 355–60). This is, perhaps, a writer's rather than a reader's way of thinking about character, but it does indicate how vividly Walker's people live in her mind.

One practical way to think about characters is to consider how they have been or might be interpreted by actors in a stage or screen adaptation. It is interesting to read Walker's notes on the characters made when she was hoping to influence Steven Spielberg's casting. She stresses physical features and postures which reflect inner states: Celie cowers in the early scenes but later when she begins 'to strut' (as Celie says, p. 126) she looks more herself and grows beautiful. Albert is small in body and mind, while Sofia is stout in body and personality (see *The Same River Twice*, pp. 51–4).

Characters often refer to aspects of their early lives that help to explain them. Sofia had to fight off her father, brothers and male cousins. 'A girl child ain't safe in a family of men,' she says (p. 38). Shug explains to Celie that she reacted against her strange mother, who hated touching people, and became sensual and strong-willed (p. 103). Harpo has been indoctrinated by his father into his belief, disastrous in his marriage to Sofia, that women must be kept in order. Albert's weakness goes back to having been dominated by his own father. Celie spends the whole novel outgrowing the exceptionally crippling experiences of her early life.

The novel teaches us that characters can change for the better under the influence of love. Celie matures through love of Shug. Albert is saved by his love for Shug from the narrow and embittering misogyny which so degrades the character of Alphonso. By the end of the story this has enabled him to grasp that Celie loves her too and they become friends.

It is sometimes suggested that a male element in a woman's character or a womanly element in a man's can be a source of strength. Celie notices that 'Shug talk and act sometimes like a man' (p. 72). Sofia takes to 'manly' activities, including outside heavy work, while Harpo enjoys child-minding and cooking. These two characters display Walker's belief that **gender** is distinct from sexual identity, and that the roles socially assigned to men and women can be destructive if they are rigidly enforced.

One technique in creating fictional characters is naming them. Shug is felt to be apter than Lillie: when she sings or makes love she is sweet as sugar. It may be that **phonaesthemic** associations with 'shush' and 'shucks' and 'shrug' and 'hug' as well as with 'sugar' ('She just so sweet they call her Shug', p. 103) give this name its strong evocative influence on our idea of what the character is like. 'Squeak' has a different and more dignified role, as a singer rather than just a little 'yellow' bargirl, when she is called Mary Agnes, and she tends to insist on her proper name. Sometimes a name is symbolic. Walker mentions that Sofia 'is named after the goddess of wisdom' (*The Same River Twice*, p. 41). How characters name or fail to name one another is also telling. It is not until the end that Celie can say 'Albert'.

Attention should also be paid, when considering character, to the voices created to bring them alive: to Shug's emphatic forms of the verb 'to be': 'it *bees* that way' (p. 10) and 'You sure *is* ugly' (p. 42), to Albert's 'Goddam' and to many other vividly individual habits of speech.

For further treatment of Celie, Shug, Albert and Nettie, see Textual Analysis. Here are some notes on the other characters:

Sofia

Sofia is a character who sometimes plays a comic role, but suffers a tragic fate. We may be amused when Harpo talks about his injuries from the barn-door and cantankerous mule; but when we hear, in Celie's recounting of Sofia's downfall, that the mayor has slapped her, we share Mary Agnes's horror at what is going to happen next to this woman of fighting spirit, in a society such as hers. That she survives her sufferings and imprisonment, and ends the novel as a dignified and courageous woman, is a symbol of the triumph of good over evil.

Mary Agnes/'Squeak'

Mary Agnes is foremost among the minor female characters. Although as Mary Agnes she gains in dignity, she seems to relapse somewhat in Grady's company, but at the end of the story she is independent once more, preparing to tour the north of the country with her new songs. She contributes to the theme of solidarity among women, in her instant concern when Sofia is arrested, and in helping to look after Sofia's children later on.

Harpo

We often sympathise with Harpo. He is to be pitied when he relives the occasion of his mother's murder in a nightmare (p. 28). We may sympathise, too, when Sofia and their children leave him. We may admire him when he rescues Albert from despair; the sight of him asleep and 'holding his daddy in his arms' makes Sofia start to 'feel again for Harpo' (p. 191). He is attractive in a different way when he recovers his spirits after Sofia's departure and sets up his jukejoint.

At other times, Harpo is a farcical figure of fun: eating six eggs for breakfast, for example, in his effort to become as big and powerful as Sofia (pp. 53–5).

Alphonso

Alphonso remarks that May Ellen, a teenage girl when he marries her after the death of Celie's mother, has left him because she 'Got too old for me I reckon' (p. 154). Her replacement is another child-wife called Daisy. He rapes Celie when she is fourteen and soon afterwards has his eye on the still younger Nettie. He particularly enjoys treating these girls as slaves. Celie is made to cut his hair just before and immediately after his violation of her. Alphonso parades her before Albert and speaks of her as though a slave for sale: 'she ain't fresh' (p. 9). He deliberately conceals the facts of their parentage from Celie and Nettie, and says in defence that knowledge of their father's fate would have upset them. He also withholds their property. 'Pa' is the least attractive of the characters.

GRADY

In Alice Walker's novels, men are (in general) the weaker sex, although not the gentler. Albert, Harpo, Alphonso and Grady exemplify male weakness and male impulses to bully. Like Harpo, Grady is to be seen as a thoughtless man who repeats unthinkingly the opinions of others. His red braces and bow ties look vulgar to Celie (because she is jealous of him). To end his days growing marijuana in Panama seems an appropriate fate for him (although not for Mary Agnes who leaves him there and returns to sing and look after her daughter).

SAMUEL AND ADAM

The Reverend Samuel and his son Adam are exceptional members of the novel's cast: they are reasonably intelligent and sensible men, and they have a positive attitude towards women. We see and hear very little of them, however, and then only through the medium of Nettie's letters. She praises Samuel first as a protector and later as a husband; she praises Adam first as a pleasant boy, later as a principled young man and the lover of Tashi; but she does not attempt the kind of dialogue and action that bring Albert and Harpo to life in Celie's letters.

CORRINE AND THE CHILDREN

We are bound to take Nettie's side, but we may also feel sorry for Corrine, whose jealousy is understandable and whose death is required by the story (since another good man for Nettie to marry might be hard to find). Nettie and Corrine have taught Olivia the progressive, liberal American views which Olivia passes on to Tashi. Tashi's difficulties, placed between the missionaries and her own people, are outlined in Nettie's letters, but remain in the distant background of the story.

THEMES

SLAVERY

Although slavery was abolished in the United States in 1865, habits of mind formed under slavery continued to degrade human relations, as the novel constantly shows. 'Girl' as a form of address (p. 76) and 'boy' meaning a servant (p. 155) are terms that date back to the era of slavery. They are still in use because the mentality has not changed. Alphonso and Albert treat women like slaves, and this is reflected in their speech: 'I can let you have Celie', 'I got a fresh one in there myself' (p. 9). The scene where Mr —, on his horse, inspects Celie, who is made to turn about in front of him, is meant to remind us of the purchase of a slave.

Miss Millie, the mayor's wife, treats Sofia as a slave, and so provokes her indignant reply, which leads to the mayor's intervention and Sofia's arrest, beating and imprisonment. It is even implied that Sofia is treated worse as a 'free' woman, when in prison, than she is when she is, in effect, the 'slave' looking after Miss Millie's children.

The theme of slavery links the African part of the story to the American. Nettie's letters express the strongest feelings for the home continent, from which the ancestors of African Americans were brought by European slave traders (pp. 114–15, for example). She is angry, however. when the Olinka refuse to discuss the slave trade (p. 140), because they are trying to hide the fact that Africans were responsible for selling slaves to European traders.

In America and in Africa, the novel insists, the inability of men to see women as equals is akin to the old slave-owning mentality, which is far from having been eradicated from the world.

EDUCATION AND LITERACY

The themes of schooling for girls' and women's writing also connect the African and American parts of the story. Nettie teaches Celie in America just as Olivia teaches Tashi in Africa, in secret, because men resent and fear the education of women. The writing of the letters, on both sides of the Atlantic, is a symbol of defiance. Albert will stop it if he can. Even though she is unaware of it, Celie's letters are from the first a record and accusation of neglect and abuse, and Nettie's letters are filled with critical observations on the incompetence and inhumanity of white colonists and of African men. Writing is seen as a weapon: for many women in the past letters offered the only available means of writing to express and share their feelings.

VIOLENCE

The fictional presentation of violence is difficult. Unsuccessful attempts to arouse pity through overinsistence on disgusting details tend to numb the reader's response. Walker's purposes in this novel require her to portray many incidents of rape and beating, but these are so tactfully described that the effect is realistic and pitiful.

Grotesque aspects of violence appear in Celie's accounts of how she has been abused (p. 97), and the inanity of violence is shown in the descriptions of Sofia's fights with Harpo (p. 36). Sofia's arrest is an extremely emotive scene: a black woman strikes a white official, and the police close in on her. The power of such an incident to arouse emotion does not make it easier to render successfully, without stereotyped effects. Celie's halting description, interrupted by Albert when she breaks down, is simple and strong. More space is given, on the next page, to Celie's caring for Sofia in prison than to her beating and arrest. *The Color Purple* depicts many scenes of violence, but it is a tender rather than a violent book.

RELIGIOUS BELIEF

'Dear God' begins each of the first fifty-one letters and the last, and 'Amen' ends Celie's letters to Nettie, as well as the novel. It is Shug who sets out explicitly the theme of 'Spirit' rather than church religion which recurs throughout the story. Celie has lost the simple but devout Christian faith which sustained her in early life because God has kept from her the knowledge of her true parentage and divided her from Nettie: she thinks God must have been asleep (p. 151). In her anger she says that 'God ... is a man', and that 'if he ever listened to poor colored women the world would be a different place I can tell you' (p. 164). Shug answers her by insisting that 'God is inside you and inside everybody else' (p. 166).

The mistake, Shug says, is to think of God as an old white man. It is better to think of the trees, and all created things. 'Man corrupt everything,' she declares. You must 'git man off your eyeball' before you can see anything (p. 168). Once the idea of God is freed from false images, however, she or he or it is to be revered and not feared because the old religious taboos, especially on sins of sex, do not apply any more. Celie is eventually converted to this new faith, and her last letter begins 'Dear God. Dear stars, dear trees, dear sky, dear peoples. Dear everything' (p. 242). Even Nettie says that 'God is different to us now ... more spirit ... and more internal' (p. 218).

Unsympathetic readers may feel that some of the religious talk in the novel is inexact, equating Spirit with matter and love with making love, but even they must admit that it is warm and sincere, and coheres with the belief that all **patriarchal** culture should be overthrown.

NARRATIVE TECHNIQUES

STRUCTURE

The story is firmly constructed, with a desperately dramatic opening, a middle full of conflict and endeavour, and a happy ending. It is a traditional type of story in beginning with the breakup of a family and ending with its reunion. The loving sisters are parted, but restored to each other in spite of all the villain's treachery. Mother and children, torn apart by cruelty, are also reunited, in happier circumstances than could ever have been expected. Virtue is further rewarded, in the cases of Celie and Nettie, by the unlooked-for and timely inheritance of house and property (hitherto wrongly withheld from them).

COINCIDENCE

Much of the action depends on coincidence: not only is Nettie befriended by the adoptive parents of Celie's children; Samuel happens (rather improbably given their respective characters and ways of life) to have been an old crony of Alphonso. Furthermore, this means that he knows the secret of the sisters' parentage. The stain of incest is thus removed; Alphonso turns out to be an evil stepfather, as we might have expected. Albert is dramatically changed into a reformed character at the end. The story may remind some readers, especially in its rather leisurely closing stages, of the ways in which Victorian **melodrama** pitted brute force against love and friendship, leaving heroes and heroines well off in every way.

Letter writing

The use of letters also contributes to the structure. It provides two points of view, and two styles, in the first-person narrators, Celie and Nettie. Letter writing (and the theft of letters) is part of the story. Each of the sisters writes as an act of faith, keeping up her own spirits in difficult times, and reaching out to the other. Albert, intercepting Nettie's letters, stands in their way, as though forbidding sisterhood.

Use of letters also affects the distribution of incidents in time. The events of a few days are described in one or more of Celie's letters, and then years pass unrecorded. Some of these intervals are noted in the letters; others are not. We sometimes have to calculate the passage of time for ourselves (see Dating Events). This elliptical method is effective in dealing with the challenge Alice Walker set herself of presenting nearly forty years, from two lives spent mostly apart, in the space of a relatively short novel (about 70,000 words).

The ending

The author's contriving of her story's happy ending is rather noticeable. Corrine dies (repentant, after all her false suspicions) just in time for Nettie to marry Samuel. The sisters inherit property. Just when Celie is ready and able to welcome Nettie, the missionary family returns home. The telegram with false news of Nettie's death ensures that her homecoming will be even more of a happy surprise.

We may accept all this under the convention of the happy ending. But we may be less willing to accept incidents where the author seems to have arranged the evidence to support her themes. Tashi's father is a feeble spokesman for Africa as a man's world, and easily disposed of. Soon after quarrelling with Nettie, he refuses Western medicine and dies of malaria. Many modern African novels in English show how much subtler and tougher a tribal elder might have been, if Alice Walker had allowed. When the bishop who receives Samuel and Nettie in England proves to be foolish and feeble, we are unsurprised because he is obviously akin to Tashi's father in the novel's scheme, which always leaves Nettie in the right.

The danger is that we may feel the author is indulging 'her' characters in ways that undermine her case: we may reflect that missionary work and small businesses, women's roles in African society, and new bearings in theology, are all more difficult and more interesting than Nettie and Celie are permitted to find out. Such thoughts are liable to arise in reading the last series of letters; if that happens, the demands of the happy ending have weakened the novel's power to persuade.

In other ways, however, *The Color Purple* is effective in reworking old conventions for new purposes. Literature constantly renews itself in this way, and Alice Walker has a sure sense of how to tell a story. Not all committed writers are so good-humoured. Her sense of fun adds to many scenes: 'Folkspants, Unlimited' might have become an overworked symbolic ploy in a less deft and exuberant writer.

DATING EVENTS

We are never given the letters' dates. Celie does not record the dates she finds on Nettie's letters. Some letters tell us how many years have passed since the one before; others do not. There is sometimes a vagueness about the passage of time. This is natural: neither sister is keeping a journal. But the way Nettie's letters take us back in time is likely to make us ask ourselves about dates.

A late letter from Nettie offers an approximate date by referring to the approach of a 'big war' (p. 194); this must be late in the 1930s. Since at least two years of the war have passed by the time of Nettie's return to America, the date here must be around 1939. The war has started five letters later; this is presumably to be dated between 1939 and 1941. Nettie gives a useful clue before coming home by saying that it is nearly thirty years since she last saw Celie (p. 217), implying a date around 1912 for their parting in Letter 11. Working back from there, we may suppose that Celie marries Albert in 1911, since they have not been together long when Nettie comes to live with them, and her need to escape from Alphonso is urgent once Celie's protection is removed. Celie reports the meeting with Corrine where Olivia is said to be six years old in her tenth letter (pp. 14–16); so the first letter must belong to the period 1904–5. Celie must have been born about 1890.

We can try to work forward from the date of Celie's marriage. Harpo is then twelve (p. 13). He is seventeen when he first talks about Sofia; this must be about 1916 (p. 22). So far he has only managed to wink at Sofia in church; when they marry, her first baby is 'a big ole nursing boy', so we must allow at least another year: Harpo brings Sofia and the baby home in 1917 or 1918 (p. 32). The next letter says that Harpo and Sofia have been married three years, bringing us to about 1920; it is at least 1921 when she leaves him because they now have five children. This is about the time of Shug Avery's arrival, sick, to stay with Albert and Celie. Since Shug stays on only to persuade Albert to stop beating Celie, after her recovery, Sofia's return ought not to be more than two years later; Shug is still singing at Harpo's place then. 1924 must be the approximate date for the events of the letters covering Sofia's imprisonment (pp. 75–86). Celie says that Sofia was in prison for three years before starting to work as a maid for Miss Millie (p. 87). We are now in 1927. Two more years of Sofia's sentence have passed in the next letter when she sees her children (p. 89), making it 1929.

Shug's return at Christmas in the next letter is difficult to date. It must be some years later, although no mention is made of the passage of time. It is during this visit that Celie and Shug find the letters from Nettie. The first letter from Nettie that Celie reads says that the family are already planning to return to America. We must be well into the 1930s. That is confirmed by the fact that Sofia has been released from prison after eleven and a half years of her sentence, as we know from the letter where Celie is still angry with Albert about his suppression of the correspondence (p. 169). This is 1935 or 1936.

Nettie's encounter with Sofia (pp. 110–12), is impossible to date, if we accept this scheme. Sofia is working as Miss Millie's maid, which means a date on or after 1927. Nettie is about to leave for Africa, and it is this meeting that persuades her to go. But Olivia and Adam would be adults by this time, and they are plainly young children when first in Africa. Her earliest letters (pp. 107–12) show that Nettie leaves for Africa soon after her parting from Celie, which is about 1912. Her first letter (p. 107) is written just after Nettie's flight, and the next says that it is too soon to hope for a reply. By the next, Nettie is 'almost crazy' at having had no reply. But it is clear that weeks, or just possibly months, have passed, not years. Nettie's fourth letter (p. 110) tells us in a headnote from Celie (unique in referring to a date) that it is dated two months after the last, and Nettie is now writing from Africa.

There are other odd features of the time-scheme. Adam and Tashi are in their thirties when they marry, about 1941, yet they behave as though at an earlier stage of life. Events among the Olinka do not seem to fit such a long span of years as the novel requires. It is best to keep the calendar roughly in mind, but not to worry about it pedantically.

LANGUAGE AND STYLE

SOUTHERN DIALECT

Celie's letters are marked by dialect features. Conjugation, especially of 'be' and 'have', is jumbled. Final 's' is often irregular ('two mens', 'she say'). Archaisms still common in many dialects occur, such as the double negative, and the form 'ain't' ('She ain't never no good!'). The pronoun system is non-standard: 'us' serves for 'we' as well as 'us'; 'they' serves for 'they' and 'their'. Phonetic spellings convey the sound of speech: 'ast' for 'asked' and 'ask'. With relatively few deviations of this kind from standard grammar, Walker creates a remarkably expressive style. The text always remains easy reading, however, by contrast, say, to the rich but difficult prose in novels of the American South by William Faulkner (1897–1962). Southern American vocabulary and idioms give us the feel of everyday life. Thinking of horse-thieves or hants makes folks nervous when opening the door at night (p. 36). If hair is nappy (p. 49), it can be cornrowed (p. 51). There may be grits (p. 46) or clabber (p. 55) for breakfast or chitlins (p. 63) and souse (p. 178) for dinner. In a community where white people are few and uninteresting, skins are not black or white but black, like Shug's, or yellow like Squeak's, or bright like Sofia's. Shoes or a song or talk may be sassy (saucy). If a preacher has got his mouth on somebody (p. 40) it may be because she has the nasty woman's disease (p. 49). Other diseases are hard to be sure about, including mysterious two berkulosis (p. 40). Down at the jukejoint, they dance the moochie and some smoke reefer (pp. 102–3).

The novel shows its author's knowledge of the **oral culture** of the old South, on which all speakers can draw. When Celie tells Albert how she has coaxed the convalescent Shug into eating some breakfast, and says that nobody living can resist the smell of home-cured ham, she adds, 'If they dead they got a chance. Maybe' (p. 47), and even Albert laughs. He and Celie have heard the joke, in the same words, many times; and so has Alice Walker.

INNOCENT NARRATORS

The Color Purple can be seen as part of a long tradition of American fiction, going back to *Huckleberry Finn* (1884) by Mark Twain (pseudonym of Samuel Langhorne Clemens, 1835–1910). In novels of this kind a young or innocent narrator tells the story in dialect and uneducated English and with a much less mature understanding than the novel expects of the reader. *The Catcher in the Rye* (1951) by J.D. Salinger (b.1919) is another such work. The style of these young narrators has the attractions of lively speech. Like Twain's Huck Finn and Salinger's Holden Caulfield, the young Celie writes the early letters in a style close to the way she speaks, and although her later writing matures, it does not lose its frank appeal.

CELIE'S STYLE

The earliest letters establish her in our sympathy. They often have a breathless immediacy:

> Dear God,
>
> He act like he can't stand me no more. Say I'm evil an always up to no good. He took my other little baby, a boy this time. But I don't think he kilt it. (p. 5)

Declining to name 'him' seems natural: this is how children talk. This style adds to the concentrated impact of the opening letters, and anyway, God knows who she is talking about.

Some of the best writing in the novel comes in Celie's curt notes on the horrific world she grows up in: 'His wife died. She was kilt by her boyfriend coming home from church' (p. 6). This is how she introduces the murder of Harpo's mother, an episode more fully described in later letters. The childish brevity, which makes the killing appear more of an everyday, unremarkable incident than it later turns out to have been, sets the right tone of gratuitous violence for Celie's early vision of the world. Celie's later letters grow in fluency, in telling use of detail and in grasp of motive, but

she remains an uncomplicated, straightforward narrator. Comparison of
the first letter and the one where Celie tells Shug how Alphonso used to
abuse her (pp. 96–7) shows how her style develops. Our impression of
crudity on first reading the third paragraph of Letter 1 is dispelled as soon
as we sense the limits of the girl's vocabulary and understanding. The blunt
description conveys exactly the emotion the author wants. The later letter
puts the same incident into an adult context. In bed with Shug, Celie relives
the misery in detail, recalling how the dripping blood 'mess up' her
stocking. There is an intimacy and an air of integrity about Celie's odd
grammar in such passages: she remembers 'how much I was surprise' by the
rape, and here her dialect helps to make her real in our imagination.

Celie is a lively and witty writer. Questions run through her mind 'like
snakes' (p. 26). When Shug first appears, seriously ill but flamboyant as
usual, Celie says, 'She look like she ain't long for this world but dressed well
for the next' (p. 42); Shug is 'skinny as a bean, and her face full of eyes' (p.
51). Good touches such as these enliven Celie's letters throughout.

Celie's letters are mostly in short paragraphs full of fast-moving
action and lots of dialogue. Nettie's letters are in longer paragraphs of
standard English, tending to relate in a formal manner states of affairs in
her own family and among the Olinka people.

For more on language and style, including style in Nettie's letters, see
Textual Analysis.

Symbolism

Purple

The title points to the imaginative design. Purple is the colour of a bruise.
When Sofia has been beaten by the police she is the colour of 'an eggplant'
(p. 77). Purple is also the colour of the robes of royalty and nobility, of
Roman emperors and English lords. This is why Celie thinks it the colour
Shug Avery would choose to wear: 'She like a queen to me, so I say to
[Albert's sister] Kate, Somethin purple, maybe little red in it too' (p. 12).
Red goes with purple, in stately robes and imperial pomp. There is no
purple in the store, and even red would be too expensive for Albert; but
Celie later makes pants of purple, red, and every other bright colour. But it

is the contrast between bruised and battered victims and the queenly, triumphant figures women can become when they are free that gives *The Color Purple* its basic structure. Celie makes pants for Sofia with one leg red and the other one purple and then dreams of her wearing them and 'jumping over the moon' (p. 184). Celie has her room painted purple and red (p. 240). The colour of bruises has become the noblest of colours by the end of the novel.

Shug gives a new significance to the colour purple when she explains her religious belief to Celie, saying that 'it pisses God off if you walk by the color purple in a field somewhere and don't notice it' (p. 167). The very existence of purple is wonderful, and therefore a symbol of the wonder of existence which is the core of the new faith Shug and Celie share.

FOLKSPANTS, UNLIMITED

Pants, or trousers, are another symbol of women's emancipation. It could be said that pants and pants-making and Celie's firm 'Folkspants, Unlimited' (p. 182) create a symbol of freedom in the modern world, while quilts and quilt making, a traditional occupation allowing women to work together and share pieces of cloth among themselves, symbolise women's solidarity, past and present.

'DEAR TREES'

Roofleaf is symbolic of traditional African values and way of life (see Text 2 of Textual Analysis). Roofleaf in Africa is connected with Shug's and Celie's celebration of trees as symbols of nature and the wonder of nature. 'Dear God. Dear stars, dear trees', Celie prays at the start of the last letter.

PART FOUR

Textual Analysis

TEXT 1 (PAGES 42–5)

From:

> 'They git halfway up the step, Mr. — look up at me. Celie, he say. This here Shug Avery.'

To:

[handwritten annotation: omission of words]

> 'I wash her body, it feel like I'm praying. My hands tremble and my breath short.'

Shug Avery's first appearance, sick but too evil to die, is a good example of how vivid and dramatic Celie's terse narrative style can be.

We are accustomed by now to Celie's relating of past events in the present tense and her frequent omission of words and **morphemes** that act as grammatical markers. We may not notice, therefore, how effectively her habits of speech give these scenes qualities of immediacy and urgency for which literary devices such as such as **ellipsis** or the **historic present tense** are used elsewhere. Omission of the verb 'to be', for example, makes the sentences about Harpo and Sofia at the end of the first paragraph seem like stage directions preceding some piece of dramatic action. In the phrases describing Shug as Celie first sees her, removal of the verbs is reminiscent of the technique of **stream of consciousness** where ellipsis suggests the flow of a character's thoughts and sense impressions. It also lets us hear Celie's speaking voice: 'But he there'. Omission of grammatical markers also gives a freshness to everyday phraseology.

These are features of Celie's speech. Typographical simplifications are effective too. Dispensing with quotation marks and the convention of a new line for a new speaker produces a sense of intimacy, as Albert's and Shug's voices interrupt Celie's without formality: 'She too evil for that. Turn loose my goddam hand, she say'.

This first meeting with Shug is a turning point in Celie's life. Hitherto Celie has known Shug from a photograph and has found sisterly reassurance in her eyes. Now it is the eyes that command attention. Though feverish, they look 'mean', ready to kill a snake and not scotch it. A more evocative term still is used twice. Shug is 'more evil than my mama' and that is what keeps her alive. She is too evil to let Albert hold her hand.

This sort of evil is obviously not the usual sense of moral depravity to be seen, for example, in Alphonso. It indicates malice, as in 'an evil temper' (sometimes said of a horse), but also has a broad range of positive meaning when applied to Shug. It implies vitality (she is hard to kill), feistiness, spunk, and independence of all the world, especially men. It is the opposite of the meekness gone soft (for Nettie can be dignified in her meekness) found in women like Celie whose spirit has been crushed, or in Albert when he acts like a weak little boy. Albert's last words may be true, but she is willing to stand against the world.

This helps to explain why Shug so fascinates Celie, possessing in abundance the qualities Celie lacks and needs. But the passage makes explicit what must be grasped in interpreting the whole novel, that Celie is possessed by sexual passion for the other woman. Shug's nakedness, black and lean and to Celie astonishing, her decisiveness ('You *is* ugly'), her humour and theatricality (hand on hip), the charisma which makes her a great blues queen, all together captivate Celie and she falls in love for good. Sweetness, too, plays a part in the charisma, accounting for her name (short for 'sugar'). Sisterhood, the novel asserts, can be the conventional bond uniting Celie and Nettie, or the solidarity between Mary Agnes and Sofia, or homosexual love, whatever 'patriarchy' may have to say.

The passage also deepens the interest of Albert. Shared love of Shug will eventually reconcile Albert and Celie, though only after the love and inspiration of Shug have allowed her to rebel against him, so it is fitting that Celie should remember Albert's name and allow herself to say it here. She is usually too frightened to name him at all. Albert's devotion, even at the cost of drink and tobacco, brings out the stronger will and personality of Shug, but also reminds us that his brutal treatment of Celie is not the whole guide to his nature. The Albert of the novel differs sharply in this respect from his counterpart in the film.

We see here what an artist with words Alice Walker has made Celie and how her powers of self-expression develop as she matures. Love brings out her delight in language:

> First time I got the full sight of Shug Avery long black body with it black plum
> nipples look like her mouth, I thought I had turned into a man.
> What you staring at? she ast. Hateful. She weak as a kitten. But her mouth just pack
> with claws. (p. 45)

Imagery such as 'mouth just pack [packed] with claws' [catty in her speech] arises from the poet in Celie. A little later she says, of Shug, 'she smile, like a razor opening' (p. 51). The **alliteration** of 'b' and 'p' and 'l' in 'long black body with it black plum nipples' would have pleased D.H. Lawrence.

The novel celebrates the creativity of women, especially in music and design. Celie later regrets that she can't cook well. She constantly shows us how well she can write.

TEXT 2   (PAGES 131–3)

From:

> 'Looking over the heads of the children at the end of this tale, I saw coming slowly towards us, a large brown spiky thing as big as a room, with a dozen legs walking slowly and carefully under it.'

To:

> 'For some reason all of her bites turn into deep, runny sores, and she has a lot of trouble sleeping at night because the noises from the forest frighten her.'

Writing to Celie, soon after her arrival in Africa, Nettie describes a village ceremony and gives an outline of her daily routine:

In Nettie's letters, Alice Walker perfectly captures the style and tone of a missionary magazine of the period, careful, earnest and unassuming. All Africa and her prodigies are recorded in much the same manner, gods and insect bites alike. The correct schoolteacher's prose counterbalances the non-standard discourse of Celie's letters. Nettie's are carefully composed pieces of writing, produced at leisure. In her sister's letters, which sometimes sound as urgent as dispatches from a battle, we hear the rhythms of live speech. Although Celie's style is much more fun, Nettie's writing has its own dignity and appeal, connected with the disciplined regularity of the way of life described in this passage.

The writing is functional and makes its points clear. These often serve to interweave themes shared by the African and American parts of the story. The ceremony of delivering the roof is part of the villagers' welcome when Samuel, Corrine, Nettie and the children arrive at their African mission station. A villager has just told the Olinka tale, related by Nettie, of a greedy chief who used land assigned to the sacred roofleaf for his own private cultivation. The ritual of honouring a new roof is preserved among the people as a mark of reverence for the leaf itself. Here, in a surprising shape, is an African God. Yet Celie will not be completely surprised when she reads about it because Shug has been teaching her to see the divine in trees and in all of nature rather than in the 'patriarchal' images of Christianity.

The next letter reveals another connection, in the theme of education for girls. Nettie regrets the backwardness of the Olinka men, and Olinka women who submit to their prejudices, wherever this impedes female emancipation. For example, the villagers send boys to school but not girls. A comparison with America is spotted by the child Olivia, who makes it without hesitation: 'They're like white people at home who don't want colored people to learn'. When she sets out to educate her friend Tashi, the image of the two girls, American and African, sharing knowledge in secret under the sheltering roofleaf, in defiance of men, attractively reaffirms the theme of worldwide sisterhood.

It may occur to some readers, especially if they have read African novels about colonial encounters with traditional culture, that Nettie does not try to analyse the problems with any depth or subtlety. But this limitation (if we feel it) does not interfere with the novel's long-range, transatlantic overview of colonial Africa, or with its plain polemical purposes. Nettie reveals the problems, the indifference of the rubber company which obliterates the rooftree and offers tin-roofed huts in exchange, the remoteness of the church authorities in England, and at least one barbarity to be found in Africa, the female circumcision which Alice Walker has described and condemned elsewhere (see Other Works by Alice Walker).

Instead of solutions, Nettie offers emotions, including indignation and concern, but mostly an unyielding love, which is given to the children and in due course to Samuel, but is concentrated on her sister. 'Dear Celie … always I am writing to you', 'Dear Nettie' − these forms of address resound with the devotion that unites the two sisters. It is this bond of sisterhood, so strongly felt, shared by Shug, Sofia, Mary Agnes, Tashi and Olivia, rather than social or political analysis, that conveys the novel's hope for the future.

TEXT 3   (PAGES 175–6)

From:

'Dear Nettie,
Well, you know wherever there's a man, there's trouble.'

To:

'Amen, say Shug. Amen, amen.'

Celie is leaving Albert to live in Memphis with Shug. In the previous letter she reports how she rebelled against Albert, saying it is time 'to leave you and enter into the Creation' (p. 170). Now, it seems the Creation curses him through her lips.

Shug has persuaded Celie that trees, or anything in nature, can serve as a better image of God than a man, especially a white man. The words of her curses now come to her as though 'from the trees'. Perhaps it is her guardian 'Familiar' who speaks, or a long-repressed rage which finds utterance while she is for a few moments 'beside herself'.

The curses are not especially forceful in phraseology, but they are appropriate and the drama of the scene lends them strength. Albert's resistance adds to the drama. He speaks with remarkable conviction: 'Look at you. You black, you pore, you ugly, you a woman. Goddam, he say, you nothing at all'. Spielberg's film weakens Albert's lines at this point by omitting 'Goddam', the word Albert pauses on in feigned surprise at just what a nothing Celie is. 'Goddam' is spoken on a rising note bringing the heavy stresses on 'black', 'pore', 'ugly', 'woman' to a climax, before the dismissive falling cadence in 'you nothing at all'. Albert may be a weak man but he has a good ear for effective sentence rhythm and Celie echoes him in her final, victorious assertion, ending 'But I'm here'.

This is a crucial passage. Celie *is* here, although Albert cannot yet acknowledge her because his contempt for the concept of 'poor black ugly woman' obstructs his awareness of the person he married. The conviction Walker gets into his words serves her purpose because it shows how instinctive his contempt is. She wants the reader to believe that all men, Olinka, American, black and white, share this unthinking assumption that a woman is inferior. She mentions with approval the remark of her friend Dennis Banks that 'there is a little bit of Mister in all of us' (*The Same River*

Twice, p. 36).

This is the most powerful of all the encounters between Albert and Celie: it demonstrates very forcefully the lightly spoken ironic reversal of a common sexist saying ('Where there's a woman, there's trouble') which opens the letter. That little bit of Mister means trouble.

'Amen', meaning 'so be it', the traditional close to a Christian prayer, becomes the closing word of Celie's letters (and of the book) when she stops writing to God, in the letter where Shug speaks about the divine Spirit present everywhere, and writes to Nettie instead (pp. 164–8). Shug is allowed the last word in the present crucial letter, which proclaims that not all the male contempt in the world can reduce Celie to 'nothing at all'. 'But I'm here,' she says, and Shug says 'Amen', three times. Walker means it to be a sacred affirmation.

PART FIVE

BACKGROUND

ALICE WALKER

SHORT BIOGRAPHY

Alice Malsenior Walker was born in 1944 in Eatonton, Georgia, in the Deep South of the United States, the youngest child of a sharecropper (a tenant farmer who supplies a share of his crop to the landlord in place of rent). An accident blinded her in one eye when she was eight. She has said that she became more shy, thoughtful and studious as a result, and began to write stories.

She went to Spelman College (for black women) in Atlanta, Georgia, in 1961, transferring to Sarah Lawrence College, New York, in 1963. Here she read widely in many literatures, and took her degree in 1965. She won a writing scholarship for the following year, and in the next two decades held a series of fellowships, awards and teaching appointments, including posts at Wellesley College and Yale University. She married Melvyn R. Levanthal, a Civil Rights lawyer, in 1967; their daughter Rebecca was born in 1969; they were divorced in 1976.

The making of the film *The Color Purple* (1985), adapted from her third novel, changed her life in ways she has described in *The Same River Twice*. She worked closely with Steven Spielberg and his team. After the film's appearance she was involved in fierce controversy within the black community in the United States (see Reading *The Color Purple*, and Critical History). In 1985 she founded, with Robert Allen, a publishing company, Wild Trees Press.

It is for *The Color Purple* that Alice Walker is best known, the novel's readership greatly enlarged after the success of the film. It has become a feminist classic (and all but a sacred text), and won the admiration of countless readers, not only feminists, by the warmth and sharpness with which its author wrote about life.

OTHER WORKS BY ALICE WALKER

Walker was a prolific and successful writer from an early age. Her essay 'The Civil Rights Movement: What Good Was It?' won a prize offered by the *American Scholar* in 1967. Her first short story, 'To Hell With Dying', was also published in 1967. *Once: Poems* (1968) was followed by several other collections of her verse. Her first novel, *The Third Life of Grange Copeland*, appeared in 1970. *In Love and Trouble: Stories of Black Women* (1973) and *You Can't Keep A Good Woman Down* (1981) are collections of her short stories. Her critical studies include *Langston Hughes: American Poet* (1974).

Alice Walker was an activist in the Civil Rights Movement which fought to end segregation and to guarantee voting rights for black Americans. Her second novel, *Meridian* (1976), reflects this concern: its heroine works for the rights of poor blacks in the Deep South. Her commitment to feminism, or in her preferred term, womanism, inspired *The Color Purple* (1982) and its successors, *The Temple of My Familiar* (1989) and *Possessing the Secret of Joy* (1992), novels which continue the story of Celie's people in more recent times. The latest novel develops a concern which appears in some of Nettie's later letters in *The Color Purple*, female genital mutilation (female circumcision). Alice Walker collaborated with Pratibha Parmar to make a film, *Warrior Marks*, and to write a book (1993) of the same title, protesting against this practice.

HISTORICAL BACKGROUND

The background is the history of black people, especially women, in the southern United States in the period between the later nineteenth century and the Second World War, and in Africa during the same (colonial) period.

Alice Walker has argued that the history of black women in modern America should be seen in three stages: the first, ending in the 1930s, and the second, ending in the 1950s, can be seen in *The Color Purple*; the third period corresponds to Walker's adult lifetime. (See the interviews reported by M.H. Washington, *Black American Literature Forum*, vol. 11, 1977, pp. 22–4.)

She calls the first period a time of 'Suspended' life for women, because they were lost in a period that offered no hope of progress. It began with the aftermath of the Civil War. When the Union of the Northern states, under President Abraham Lincoln (1809–65), defeated the Confederacy of Southern states in 1865, slavery was abolished throughout the United States by the 13th Amendment to the Constitution, ratified in December 1865. The 14th Amendment of the following year granted citizenship and equal civil rights to the four million ex-slaves. The 15th Amendment reinforced the right of all Americans to vote, in 1870. Northerners felt satisfied with these measures, and did not closely concern themselves with what actually took place in the South. The economy and social order of the former slave-states had been shattered by the war. Although black people were free, they were still poor, and easy targets for injustice. Although black men could legally own property and exercise power, as we see in *The Color Purple*, their right to hold property was in effect precarious; they had little hope of redress when it was taken from them. The father of Celie and Nettie was lynched because his business had become a threat to his white rivals. The condition of women was little changed. They laboured in the fields as before, and were, in a phrase of the black woman novelist Zora Neale Hurston that Walker often quotes, 'the mules of the world', laden with every sort of social burden. The reader is shown how these women toiled, insulted and abused by men, black and white. In *The Third Life of Grange Copeland* (1970) and in *The Color Purple* (1982), Alice Walker has been particularly concerned to emphasise the stifling of creative talent in the women of this unhappy era.

The women of Alice Walker's second historical phase are said to have been 'assimilated', during the 1940s and 1950s, 'into the mainstream of American life'. This brought a danger of separation from their ethnic background. In the closing stages of *The Color Purple*, the principal female characters, Celie, Shug, Sofia and Mary Agnes, are free from the 'suspended' condition of drudgery in which they were all born at the end of the nineteenth century, and are prospering as professional singers and businesswomen in the early 1940s. The positive side of their achievement is highlighted in this novel, but we see signs of difficulty in race relations in Sofia's troubled dealings with the white woman Eleanor Jane.

Walker's third phase, a time of 'emergent' women, began with the Civil Rights Movement of the 1960s, although thoroughly liberated women belonging to earlier periods appear in her novels; we might consider Shug Avery in *The Color Purple* to be one of them. The novelist herself certainly corresponds to her own definition of a woman of this latest age, 'called to life' by the struggles of the 1960s to fight segregation on buses and in restaurants and to achieve full equality for black citizens. The essays of *In Search of Our Mothers' Gardens* include a tribute to Dr Martin Luther King (1929–68), the orator and moral leader of the Movement. Walker emphasises in many essays that the Movement changed human attitudes in the American South. The outlook of her mother, who brought up eight children of her own and lots more besides, and believed that black people were inferior to white, belongs to the 'Suspended' era of the past (*In Search of Our Mothers' Gardens*, p. 123).

The Women's Movement is the other modern movement that has deeply influenced Alice Walker, and it has become her foremost commitment. Her loyalties were divided when she was obliged to criticise sexism among fellow Civil Rights activists. Her second novel, *Meridian* (1976), depicts a highly principled young woman, working in the Civil Rights Movement, who adopts a peaceful but feminist programme in place of the masculine goal of violent revolution. By the time she wrote *The Color Purple*, Walker had decided that she must risk male hostility by an unswerving commitment to the plight of black women abused by men of their own race.

The African setting of the novel is less precisely located than the scenes in Georgia and Tennessee. The heroine's sister Nettie is a missionary in West Africa between about 1914 and about 1941. Most of the continent was then under colonial rule. We hear of the Belgian Congo and of Senegal, where the boat taking Nettie out from England makes a stop at the then French-colonial capital, Dakar. Her next stop is in Liberia, which was an independent state created in the nineteenth century as a refuge for black immigrants returning to Africa from the United States. Rubber planting in the territory of the Olinka people, among whom Nettie works in the novel, suggests a setting in Liberia, where rubber was extensively introduced in the 1920s. But Nettie has sailed on from Liberia and seems, from the stamps on her letters and other indications, to be in a British colony. The ruthless character of the road-building and rubber-planting which destroy the homes, fields and way of life of the Olinka are clearly intended to show the treatment of African peoples under colonialism throughout the continent, and not merely one particular case of bad administration.

Religious practice and beliefs are another feature of the background. Protestant Christianity was quickly absorbed into the culture brought to America from Africa during the era of slavery (from the seventeenth to the nineteenth century). Fostered by songs, music and passionate preaching, the Christian faith remained strong among black people after Emancipation. The appeal of 'the black church' to its women can be seen in *The Third Life of Grange Copeland* (1970) and in *Meridian* (1976). It has been suggested that Southern Baptist sermons may have influenced Walker's choice of the form of letters to God for her third novel, since it was common for preachers to tell of their talks with the Lord, and Celie would have heard them.

Most of the novel is set in the golden age of jazz and blues singing. 'Duke' Ellington (1899–1974) and Bessie Smith (1894–1937) are among the great artists and entertainers mentioned. The great jazz and blues singers of the time managed to reflect ordinary life in their songs. Furthermore, the independent, flamboyant lives of these women were in stark contrast to those of women like Celie. In the character of Shug Avery, we see a reflection of their flair and creative spirit.

LITERARY BACKGROUND

Alice Walker is among the best known and most admired of the many black women novelists from the South of the United States whose work has been published during the last twenty years, a group that includes Toni Morrison (see Further Reading). Earlier writers who influenced this new school of novelists, and Alice Walker in particular, are Zora Neale Hurston, whose novel *Their Eyes Were Watching God* (Harper Collins, 1995) first appeared in 1937, and Margaret Walker (b.1915), author of the epic novel of black American life, *Jubilee* (Bantam, 1995, originally published 1966). Walker calls Zora Neale Hurston (whom she has written about and edited) her 'literary progenitor'. She admires Hurston's 'complete, undiminished sense of self'. She has aimed to imitate Hurston's ability 'to let her characters be themselves, funny talk and all', and she admires the way that Hurston was 'incapable of being embarrassed by anything black people did, and so was able to write about everything' (*In Search of Our Mothers' Gardens*, p. 259).

Among other black American writers who have influenced her work, she mentions with special praise Jean Toomer (1894–1967), poet, playwright and fiction-writer, whose novel *Cane* (Norton, 1988, originally published 1923) was a major work of the movement called the Harlem Renaissance; and the poet, songwriter, playwright, novelist and musician Langston Hughes (1902–67), whom Toomer influenced, and about whom Walker has written a book. She notes of Toomer that 'he has a very feminine sensibility', adding 'unlike most black male writers' *(In Search of Our Mothers' Gardens*, p. 259).

Alice Walker has acknowledged the influence of many writers in other traditions. Among white women writers she admires are the Brontë sisters, Anne (1820–49), Charlotte (1816–55) and Emily (1818–48); Doris Lessing (b.1919), whose work draws on her upbringing in Zimbabwe (then Southern Rhodesia), and whose novel *The Golden Notebook* (Paladin 1989, originally published 1962) treats themes from feminist points of view; and Simone de Beauvoir (1908–86), the French novelist and essayist, author of a key feminist work, translated as *The Second Sex* (translated by H.M. Parshley, Picador, 1988, originally published as *Le deuxième sexe*, 1949). She says of this group of writers that 'well aware of their own oppression', they use their gifts as creative writers to fulfil themselves as women (*In Search of Our Mothers' Gardens*, p. 251).

As a student, Walker read all the Russian novels she could. She learned from Leo Tolstoy (1828–1910) 'to drive through' political and social issues to reach the individual spirit, an effort needed to make characters live (*In Search of Our Mothers' Gardens*, p. 257). She admired the other great Russians of the nineteenth century, but was disappointed to find no Russian women novelists. Among poets, she enjoyed the Americans Emily Dickinson (1830–86) and e.e. cummings (1894–1962), and the British poet Robert Graves (1895–1985), champion of the White (Moon) Goddess, who represents the creative female principle, long suppressed by male rationalising (*In Search of Our Mothers' Gardens*, p. 257). *The Temple of My Familiar* is dedicated 'To Robert, in whom the Goddess shines'. She also speaks of her enjoyment of the 'sensual' Latin poems of Catullus (*c.*84–*c.*54BC) and Ovid (43BC–AD17), and of Japanese haiku poets who taught her the possibilities of short forms.

Among African writers, she praises the Nigerian, Elechi Amadi (b.1934), whose novel *The Concubine* (1966) may have influenced her story 'Roselily', a prototype of *The Color Purple,* and the distinguished South African novelist Bessie Head (1937–86), whose conviction that God is known in Africa in ways undreamt of by missionaries may have influenced the presentation of religious themes in Walker's fiction.

The Color Purple belongs to the genre of **epistolary** novels. The greatest writer in this tradition was one of the earliest, Samuel Richardson (1689–1761). The novel in letters appealed to women novelists, including Mrs Aphra Behn (1640–89) and Fanny Burney (1752–1840). Jane Austen (1775–1817) also experimented with novels in the form of letters. There have been novels of this kind in the modern period, but the invention of the telephone seems to have impaired the already somewhat restricted nature of the genre. Alice Walker may have had in mind her predecessors among female novelists, but she may also have intended to remind us of Richardson's vast and enthralling novels *Pamela* (1740–1) and *Clarissa* (1747–8), which deal with the plight of women insulted and abused by villainous men. Like Jean Toomer, Richardson was a man with a strong and delicate sensibility.

PART SIX

C RITICAL HISTORY

The Color Purple quickly divided intellectual opinion among African Americans. Many men attacked the book and the film on political grounds, arguing that the stress on violence and cruelty in the portrayal of the central black male characters threatened the unity of the African American community and its struggle for civil rights. In *The Same River Twice* Alice Walker reprints some of the attacks (she was denounced as 'a liar, a whore, a traitor'), including an article in the *Carolina Peacemaker* in 1986 which endorsed *Time*'s summary, 'Walker's message: "Sisterhood is beautiful and Men stink"' (p. 224). In mounting her defence, Walker became perhaps the novel's most prolific and interesting interpreter. *The Same River Twice* reprints sympathetic reviews, dozens of enthusiastic letters from readers, offers views on various aspects of the novel, and gives a detailed account of Walker's involvement in the making of the film (including her screenplay, rejected by Spielberg).

One recurring theme in this volume is Walker's disappointment at Spielberg's having all but excluded the lesbian relationship (leaving only one kiss), and another is that Albert is portrayed 'unforgivingly', that is, as a wholly unsympathetic character. The Albert of the novel, she insists, is a complex and many-layered creation, written from love of the spirit of black men (a spirit alive in herself) as well as from hatred of male abuse of women.

Among black women, critics have not always been well disposed. A notable adverse critic is bell hooks, whose essay of 1990 (see Further Reading) attacks the novel for failing to present its lesbian theme in an adequate political framework. Celie's relationship with Shug is seen as a purely personal affair, which provokes none of the hostility that homosexuality often arouses in modern society. Furthermore, Shug and Celie succeed in business by accepting the heterosexual and capitalist society about them. It could be said that they surrender to 'the American Dream'. hooks's is a thoughtful article written from a more radical feminist position than Alice Walker's.

Many of the most interesting interpretations in recent years have come from feminists. One area of disagreement concerns the concept of realism. A particularly good critical essay is Andrea Stuart's '*The Color Purple*: In Defence of Happy Endings' in *The Female Gaze* (1988). Stuart defends the novel against charges that the plot is too dependent on coincidences and that the concept of spirit is inadequate ('wishy-washy') by arguing that it should be read not as 'a realist novel in the ordinary sense' but rather as a folk tale or a fable in the tradition of the Uncle Remus stories (see Summary on Letter 64) 'which advocate tolerance, patience, perseverance and cunning for the underdog's survival' (p. 65).

Others disagree. bell hooks insists that Walker has committed herself to the realist tradition going back to the early 'slave narratives' and black protest writing in the nineteenth century, which aimed to tell the truth about slavery and its aftermath. Conditions among black women in early-twentieth-century America, *The Color Purple* declares, really were as the novel portrays them, with no admixture of fantasy or fable-making or Uncle Remus. hooks acknowledges this realist commitment but objects that it is betrayed by the happy ending, which buries the public issues in the characters' private emotions. What of Sofia, the revolutionary, for whom there is no happy ending?

Renée C. Hoogland supports bell hooks in reading the novel 'in the tradition of social realism'. Noting that violet and lavender were emblematic of lesbianism in antiquity, Hoogland argues that Walker fails to be realistic enough because she does not understand the implications of her lesbian theme. Shug and Celie are content to enjoy their relationship in private, without challenging the patriarchal and heterosexual society about them.

The central place the novel has won in women's studies can be seen from a collection called *Women's Studies and Culture: A Feminist Introduction* (1995), where Hoogland's article appears. This volume includes essays on literary theory, history, film studies, art history, musicology, lesbian studies and semiotics, all of which discuss *The Color Purple*.

Some of these essays point out that not all Alice Walker's basic assumptions are very different from old patriarchal ones, such as belief in human nature, and in the transforming power of love. Nor is she very radical in her critical conceptions. She believes in fictional characters with their own odd kind of reality, and in authors with intentions that readers can get right or wrong. Where conventional readers have been shocked by the novel, several recent critics have seen Walker as a traditional humanist. Liesbeth Brouwer, writing in *Women's Studies and Culture*, finds *The Color Purple* 'the perfect emancipation novel', but also 'a novel which inscribes women in a familiar tale: it reproduces the modernist [here meaning traditional] and liberal democratic ideology which defines a task for women and men alike, that is, to strive for a fulfilled life' (p. 158).

PART SEVEN

B ROADER PERSPECTIVES

F URTHER READING

Alice Walker's books are all published in New York by Harcourt Brace Jovanovich, and in London by The Women's Press. Students of *The Color Purple* might go on to read the sequels, *The Temple of My Familiar*, 1989 and *Possessing the Secret of Joy*, 1992. It is strongly recommended, however, that you read, or at least dip into, Walker's book of essays, *In Search of Our Mothers' Gardens: Womanist Prose* (1983). *The Same River Twice: Honoring the Difficult: A Meditation on Life, Spirit, Art, and the Making of the Film The Color Purple Ten Years Later* (1996) is also full of relevant and interesting ideas.

For an introduction to Zora Neale Hurston, the black American writer to whom Alice Walker is most indebted, see Walker's own selection, *I Love Myself When I am Laughing: A Zora Neale Hurston Reader* (Feminist Press, New York, 1979). For further reading in modern American fiction by black women, try Toni Morrison. *The Bluest Eye (1970), Sula* (1973) and *Tar Baby* (1981) are published by Chatto and Windus, London.

To make a start on African fiction in English, try *Things Fall Apart*, (Heinemann, London, 1958) by Chinua Achebe.

For a critical essay in appreciation of the novel and a discussion of the film, read '*The Color Purple*: In Defence of Happy Endings' by Andrea Stuart in Gamman L. and Marshment M. (Eds), *The Female Gaze: Women as Viewers of Popular Culture* (The Women's Press, London, 1988). bell hooks's essay of 1990, 'Writing the Subject: Reading *The Color Purple*', is in Henry Louis Gates Jnr (Ed.), *Reading Black, Reading Feminist: A Critical Anthology* (Meridian, New York, 1990). Renée C. Hoogland's essay, 'Heterosexual Screening: Lesbian Studies', appears in Buikema R. and Smelik A. (Eds), *Women's Studies and Culture: A Feminist Introduction* (Zed Books, London and New Jersey, 1995). This collection, which first appeared in Dutch in 1993, includes Liesbeth Brouwer's essay, 'The Colour of the Sign: Feminist semiotics', quoted in Critical History, and other discussions of *The Color Purple* from several feminist viewpoints, including literary theory, linguistics, film studies, art history and musicology.

For information about women's involvement in the struggle to end slavery in the nineteenth century, slave narratives and the famous 'Ain't I a Woman?' speech by Sojourner Truth, see *Women, Race and Class* (The Women's Press, 1982), by Angela Davis.

CHRONOLOGY

World events	Alice Walker	Literary events
		1740-1 Samuel Richardson, *Pamela*

World events

1822 Liberia is founded as a colony for freed slaves

1834 Slavery is abolished in the British Empire

1841 David Livingstone begins missionary work in Africa

1857 Dakar founded

1858 John Hanning Speke becomes first European to see Lake Victoria

1861 Civil war breaks out in North America

1865 End of the American Civil War; slavery is abolished in the USA

1866 Ex-slaves granted citizenship and equal rights; Ku Klux Klan founded

1871 Henry Morton Stanley finds David Livingstone near Lake Tanganyika

1884-1966 Sophie Tucker, black American singer, actress and entertainer

1890-1912 Various Southern States pass 'Jim Crow' laws to segregate whites and blacks; all Southern States passed laws imposing requirements for voting that were used to prevent blacks from voting

1894-1937 Bessie Smith, black American singer

1899-1974 Duke Ellington, black American bandleader

Literary events

1740-1 Samuel Richardson, *Pamela*

1851-2 Harriet Beecher Stowe, *Uncle Tom's Cabin*

1881-1910 Joel Chandler Harris, *Uncle Remus* series

1884 Mark Twain, *Huckleberry Finn*

1903 W.E.B. Du Bois, *The Souls of Black Folk*

World events	Alice Walker	Literary events
1905 Niagra movement founded in the USA		
1908 Belgium takes possession of Belgian Congo		
1909 National Association for the Advancement of Colored People founded in the USA		
1914-18 World War I - blacks were enlisted to fight for the USA, though they were still segregated		
1929 Wall Street Crash		**1923** Jean Toomer, *Cane*
1930 The black nationalist separatist organisation, The Nation of Islam, is founded		
		1937 Zora Neale Hurston, *Their Eyes Were Watching God*
1938 Supreme Court ruled that the state of Missouri was obliged to provide access to a public law school for blacks, just as it provided for whites		
	1944 Born in Eatonton, Georgia	
		1949 Simone de Beauvoir, *The Second Sex*
		1951 J.D. Salinger, *The Catcher in the Rye*
1954 Supreme Court stated that racially segregated education was unconstitutional		
1956 In Montgomery, Alabama, Rosa Parks refuses to give up her bus seat to a white man leading to mass boycotts and the start of the Civil Rights Movement		
1957 Martin Luther King becomes president of the newly founded Southern Christian Leadership Conference		

World events	Alice Walker	Literary events
		1959 Lorraine Vivian Hansberry, *A Raisin in the Sun*
	1961 Begins studies at Spelman College, Atlanta, Georgia	
		1962 Doris Lessing, *The Golden Notebook*
	1963 Transfers to Sarah Lawrence College, New York	
1964 Congress passes the Civil Rights Act banning segregation		
1965 Race riots occur throughout the USA in protest against economic and social conditions; USA sends troops to Vietnam	**1965** Graduates; wins writing scholarship for following year	
		1966 Margaret Walker, *Jubilee;* Elechi Amadi, *The Concubine*
	1967 Marries Melvyn R. Levanthal, a Civil Rights lawyer; Alice's essay *The Civil Rights Movement: What Good Was It?* wins a prize offered by American Scholar; publishes her first short story *To Hell With Dying*	
1968 Martin Luther King is assassinated; the militant Black Panther organisation is founded to promote the armed self protection of black communities	**1968** Publishes her first collection of poems, *Once: Poems*	
	1969 Rebecca, her daughter, is born	
	1970 Publishes her first novel, *The Third Life of Grange Copeland*	**1970** Toni Morrison, *The Bluest Eye*
1972 Equal Opportunity Act leads to extension of affirmative action to colleges and universities		

World events	Alice Walker	Literary events
	1973 *Love and Trouble: Stories of Black Women*	**1973** Toni Morrison, *Sula*
1974 Nixon resigns	**1974** *Langston Hughes: American Poet*	
1975 USA withdraws from Vietnam		
1976 Riots in Soweto, South Africa	**1976** Alice and Melvyn are divorced; *Meridian*	
1977 Public Works Employment Act ensures 10% of contractors on public works must be from minorities		**1977** Ama Ata Aidoo, *Our Sister Killjoy*
	1981 *You Can't Keep a Good Woman Down*	**1981** Toni Morrison, *Tar Baby*
	1982 *The Color Purple* is published	**1982** Gloria Naylor, *The Women of Brewster Place*
	1983 *In Search of Our Mothers' Gardens: Womanist Prose;* becomes first black woman to win the Pulitzer Prize for literature	
	1985 Steven Spielberg's film of *The Color Purple* opens; co-founds Wild Trees Press publishing company	
		1987 Toni Morrison, *Beloved*
	1989 *The Temple of My Familiar*	**1989** Buchi Emecheta, *Gwendolen*
1990 Nelson Mandela released from twenty-seven years imprisonment		
	1992 *Possessing the Secret of Joy*	**1992** Toni Morrison, *Jazz and Playing in the Dark: Whiteness* and *the Literary Imagination*
	1993 *Warrior Marks* (book and film) with Pratibha Parmer	
1994 Nelson Mandela becomes President of South Africa		

alliteration a pattern in which one consonant is repeated, as in 'Five miles meandering with a mazy motion', or two or more alternate, as in 'And rents were lower in Rawlinson Road'

black today a cultural and political term, which makes no reference to skin colour, although it sometimes does so refer in the speech of characters in the novel

closure the sense of an ending, happy, tragic or thoughtful, which marks the close of a story or play; deliberately unfinished or unresolved stories are sometimes said to be 'open-ended'

ellipsis omission of words normally required by grammar for literary effect, as in 'He for God only, she for God in him', where the verbs are missing

epistolary in the form of letters

gender in feminist writings, now refers to sexual identity seen as the product of social and cultural influences, rather than to biological difference

historic present (tense) use of present tense to relate past events to create a sense of immediacy

imagery an image is (i) a picture created by words, as in 'the image of Olivia passing on her lessons to Tashi' (ii) a metaphor or a simile, as in 'She smile, like a razor opening'

melodrama a sensational story with violent and improbable events

morpheme the smallest meaningful unit of speech, either a word, such as 'fair' or a part of a word such as 'un' in 'unfair' or 'ly' in 'fairly'

oral culture one in which myths and legends, jokes and proverbs, folk tales and ballads and all components of the culture are remembered and repeated rather than written down

pantheist believes that God is in everything or that God is the universe. In America, Ralph Waldo Emerson (1803–82) spread belief in an ultimate spiritual revelation of the union of mind and nature, in opposition to the Christian belief that God created nature

patriarchy originally, rule by the fathers (of the tribe). In feminist criticism, refers to ways in which culture is organised according to masculine values

phonaesthemic relating sound and meaning through association. The monosyllabic phonaestheme 'Shug' may be grouped with 'shove', 'shun', 'shush', 'shut', 'shuffle', 'shucks', or with a group including 'shrug' or another including 'hug', to try to identify an English-speaker's feeling for the name

point of view in first-person narratives the narrator, usually one of the characters, tells the story from his or her point of view, using 'I'. In a novel in letters, the point of view changes with the letter-writer

realism a tendency, strong in nineteenth-century novels, sceptically regarded by many modern writers, to aim to convey the actual experience of ordinary life. It can thought of as the opposite of fantasy or escapism. It is, however, a flexible and slippery term

rhetoric(al) devices in the art of public speaking, often suspect in Western culture today, but respected in Africa and by African-American preachers and politicians. 'Ain't I a woman?', reiterated in Sojourner Truth's famous speech, was a rhetorical question, since everyone could see that she was

slave narrative the autobiography of a former slave. See *Six Women's Slave Narratives* (Oxford University Press, New York and Oxford, 1988)

stream of consciousness a technique in modern narrative which abandons composition in properly formed sentences in order to try to catch the flow of a character's thoughts and feelings

A UTHOR OF THIS NOTE

Neil McEwan read English at Pembroke College, Oxford, and now teaches in the English Department at Nara Women's University, Japan. He has published several critical studies, including *The Survival of the Novel* (1981), *Africa and the Novel* (1983), *Perspective in British Historical Fiction Today* (1987), and *Graham Greene* (1988) and *Anthony Powell* (1991) in the 'Macmillan Modern Novelists' series. He edited Volume 5, *The Twentieth Century,* in *The Macmillan Anthologies of English Literature* (1989). He is the author of *Style in English Prose* (1986) and *Preparing for Examinations in English Literature* (1982) in York Handbooks.

NOTES

NOTES

Notes

York Notes Advanced (£3.99 each)

Margaret Atwood
The Handmaid's Tale

Jane Austen
Mansfield Park

Jane Austen
Persuasion

Jane Austen
Pride and Prejudice

Alan Bennett
Talking Heads

William Blake
Songs of Innocence and of Experience

Charlotte Brontë
Jane Eyre

Emily Brontë
Wuthering Heights

Geoffrey Chaucer
The Franklin's Tale

Geoffrey Chaucer
General Prologue to the Canterbury Tales

Geoffrey Chaucer
The Wife of Bath's Prologue and Tale

Joseph Conrad
Heart of Darkness

Charles Dickens
Great Expectations

John Donne
Selected Poems

George Eliot
The Mill on the Floss

F. Scott Fitzgerald
The Great Gatsby

E.M. Forster
A Passage to India

Brian Friel
Translations

Thomas Hardy
The Mayor of Casterbridge

Thomas Hardy
Tess of the d'Urbervilles

Seamus Heaney
Selected Poems from Opened Ground

Nathaniel Hawthorne
The Scarlet Letter

James Joyce
Dubliners

John Keats
Selected Poems

Christopher Marlowe
Doctor Faustus

Arthur Miller
Death of a Salesman

Toni Morrison
Beloved

William Shakespeare
Antony and Cleopatra

William Shakespeare
As You Like It

William Shakespeare
Hamlet

William Shakespeare
King Lear

William Shakespeare
Measure for Measure

William Shakespeare
The Merchant of Venice

William Shakespeare
Much Ado About Nothing

William Shakespeare
Othello

William Shakespeare
Romeo and Juliet

William Shakespeare
The Tempest

William Shakespeare
The Winter's Tale

Mary Shelley
Frankenstein

Alice Walker
The Color Purple

Oscar Wilde
The Importance of Being Earnest

Tennessee Williams
A Streetcar Named Desire

John Webster
The Duchess of Malfi

W.B. Yeats
Selected Poems

GCSE and equivalent levels (£3.50 each)

Maya Angelou
I Know Why the Caged Bird Sings

Jane Austen
Pride and Prejudice

Alan Ayckbourn
Absent Friends

Elizabeth Barrett Browning
Selected Poems

Robert Bolt
A Man for All Seasons

Harold Brighouse
Hobson's Choice

Charlotte Brontë
Jane Eyre

Emily Brontë
Wuthering Heights

Shelagh Delaney
A Taste of Honey

Charles Dickens
David Copperfield

Charles Dickens
Great Expectations

Charles Dickens
Hard Times

Charles Dickens
Oliver Twist

Roddy Doyle
Paddy Clarke Ha Ha Ha

George Eliot
Silas Marner

George Eliot
The Mill on the Floss

William Golding
Lord of the Flies

Oliver Goldsmith
She Stoops To Conquer

Willis Hall
The Long and the Short and the Tall

Thomas Hardy
Far from the Madding Crowd

Thomas Hardy
The Mayor of Casterbridge

Thomas Hardy
Tess of the d'Urbervilles

Thomas Hardy
The Withered Arm and other Wessex Tales

L.P. Hartley
The Go-Between

Seamus Heaney
Selected Poems

Susan Hill
I'm the King of the Castle

Barry Hines
A Kestrel for a Knave

Louise Lawrence
Children of the Dust

Harper Lee
To Kill a Mockingbird

Laurie Lee
Cider with Rosie

Arthur Miller
The Crucible

Arthur Miller
A View from the Bridge

Robert O'Brien
Z for Zachariah

Frank O'Connor
My Oedipus Complex and other stories

George Orwell
Animal Farm

J.B. Priestley
An Inspector Calls

Willy Russell
Educating Rita

Willy Russell
Our Day Out

J.D. Salinger
The Catcher in the Rye

William Shakespeare
Henry IV Part 1

William Shakespeare
Henry V

William Shakespeare
Julius Caesar

William Shakespeare
Macbeth

William Shakespeare
The Merchant of Venice

William Shakespeare
A Midsummer Night's Dream

William Shakespeare
Much Ado About Nothing

William Shakespeare
Romeo and Juliet

William Shakespeare
The Tempest

William Shakespeare
Twelfth Night

George Bernard Shaw
Pygmalion

Mary Shelley
Frankenstein

R.C. Sherriff
Journey's End

Rukshana Smith
Salt on the snow

John Steinbeck
Of Mice and Men

Robert Louis Stevenson
Dr Jekyll and Mr Hyde

Jonathan Swift
Gulliver's Travels

Robert Swindells
Daz 4 Zoe

Mildred D. Taylor
Roll of Thunder, Hear My Cry

Mark Twain
Huckleberry Finn

James Watson
Talking in Whispers

William Wordsworth
Selected Poems

A Choice of Poets

Mystery Stories of the Nineteenth Century including The Signalman

Nineteenth Century Short Stories

Poetry of the First World War

Six Women Poets

FUTURE TITLES IN THE YORK NOTES SERIES

Chinua Achebe
Things Fall Apart

Edward Albee
Who's Afraid of Virginia Woolf?

Margaret Atwood
Cat's Eye

Jane Austen
Emma

Jane Austen
Northanger Abbey

Jane Austen
Sense and Sensibility

Samuel Beckett
Waiting for Godot

Robert Browning
Selected Poems

Robert Burns
Selected Poems

Angela Carter
Nights at the Circus

Geoffrey Chaucer
The Merchant's Tale

Geoffrey Chaucer
The Miller's Tale

Geoffrey Chaucer
The Nun's Priest's Tale

Samuel Taylor Coleridge
Selected Poems

Daniel Defoe
Moll Flanders

Daniel Defoe
Robinson Crusoe

Charles Dickens
Bleak House

Charles Dickens
Hard Times

Emily Dickinson
Selected Poems

Carol Ann Duffy
Selected Poems

George Eliot
Middlemarch

T.S. Eliot
The Waste Land

T.S. Eliot
Selected Poems

Henry Fielding
Joseph Andrews

E.M. Forster
Howards End

John Fowles
The French Lieutenant's Woman

Robert Frost
Selected Poems

Elizabeth Gaskell
North and South

Stella Gibbons
Cold Comfort Farm

Graham Greene
Brighton Rock

Thomas Hardy
Jude the Obscure

Thomas Hardy
Selected Poems

Joseph Heller
Catch-22

Homer
The Iliad

Homer
The Odyssey

Gerard Manley Hopkins
Selected Poems

Aldous Huxley
Brave New World

Kazuo Ishiguro
The Remains of the Day

Ben Jonson
The Alchemist

Ben Jonson
Volpone

James Joyce
A Portrait of the Artist as a Young Man

Philip Larkin
Selected Poems

D.H. Lawrence
The Rainbow

D.H. Lawrence
Selected Stories

D.H. Lawrence
Sons and Lovers

D.H. Lawrence
Women in Love

John Milton
Paradise Lost Bks I & II

John Milton
Paradise Lost Bks IV & IX

Thomas More
Utopia

Sean O'Casey
Juno and the Paycock

George Orwell
Nineteen Eighty-four

John Osborne
Look Back in Anger

Wilfred Owen
Selected Poems

Sylvia Plath
Selected Poems

Alexander Pope
Rape of the Lock and other poems

Ruth Prawer Jhabvala
Heat and Dust

Jean Rhys
Wide Sargasso Sea

William Shakespeare
As You Like It

William Shakespeare
Coriolanus

William Shakespeare
Henry IV Pt 1

William Shakespeare
Henry V

William Shakespeare
Julius Caesar

William Shakespeare
Macbeth

William Shakespeare
Measure for Measure

William Shakespeare
A Midsummer Night's Dream

William Shakespeare
Richard II

William Shakespeare
Richard III

William Shakespeare
Sonnets

William Shakespeare
The Taming of the Shrew

William Shakespeare
Twelfth Night

William Shakespeare
The Winter's Tale

George Bernard Shaw
Arms and the Man

George Bernard Shaw
Saint Joan

Muriel Spark
The Prime of Miss Jean Brodie

John Steinbeck
The Grapes of Wrath

John Steinbeck
The Pearl

Tom Stoppard
Arcadia

Tom Stoppard
Rosencrantz and Guildenstern are Dead

Jonathan Swift
Gulliver's Travels and The Modest Proposal

Alfred, Lord Tennyson
Selected Poems

W.M. Thackeray
Vanity Fair

Virgil
The Aeneid

Edith Wharton
The Age of Innocence

Tennessee Williams
Cat on a Hot Tin Roof

Tennessee Williams
The Glass Menagerie

Virginia Woolf
Mrs Dalloway

Virginia Woolf
To the Lighthouse

William Wordsworth
Selected Poems

Metaphysical Poets

York Notes – the Ultimate Literature Guides

York Notes are recognised as the best literature study guides. If you have enjoyed using this book and have found it useful, you can now order others directly from us – simply follow the ordering instructions below.

HOW TO ORDER

Decide which title(s) you require and then order in one of the following ways:

Booksellers
All titles available from good bookstores.

By post
List the title(s) you require in the space provided overleaf, select your method of payment, complete your name and address details and return your completed order form and payment to:

> *Addison Wesley Longman Ltd*
> *PO BOX 88*
> *Harlow*
> *Essex CM19 5SR*

By phone
Call our Customer Information Centre on 01279 623923 to place your order, quoting mail number: HEYN1.

By fax
Complete the order form overleaf, ensuring you fill in your name and address details and method of payment, and fax it to us on 01279 414130.

By e-mail
E-mail your order to us on awlhe.orders@awl.co.uk listing title(s) and quantity required and providing full name and address details as requested overleaf. Please quote mail number: HEYN1. Please do not send credit card details by e-mail.

York Notes Order Form

Titles required:

Quantity	Title/ISBN	Price

Sub total _____

Please add £2.50 postage & packing _____

(*P & P is free for orders over £50*) _____

Total _____

| Mail no: HEYN1 |

Your Name _____

Your Address _____

_____

Postcode _____ Telephone _____

Method of payment

☐ I enclose a cheque or a P/O for £_____ made payable to Addison Wesley Longman Ltd

☐ Please charge my Visa/Access/AMEX/Diners Club card
Number _____ Expiry Date _____
Signature _____ Date _____

(please ensure that the address given above is the same as for your credit card)

Prices and other details are correct at time of going to press but may change without notice. All orders are subject to status.

☐ *Please tick this box if you would like a complete listing of Longman Study Guides (suitable for GCSE and A-level students)*

🌐 York Press

📘 Longman

Addison Wesley Longman